1914
GLORY DEPARTING

EDWARD OWEN

880566

BUCHAN & ENRIGHT, PUBLISHERS
LONDON

First published in 1986 by
Buchan & Enright, Publishers, Limited
53 Fleet Street, London EC4Y 1BE

British Library Cataloguing in Publication Data

Owen, Edward
    1914: glory departing
    1. World War 1914–1918
    I. Title
    940.3   D521

ISBN 0-907675-38-7

Photoset in North Wales by
Derek Doyle & Associates, Mold, Clwyd
Printed in Great Britain by
Biddles Ltd, Guildford

CONTENTS

For Gwnedd,
who remembers,
and of course
for Muriel

ILLUSTRATIONS

MAPS

Drawn by Neil Hyslop

PREFACE

This is a book largely about what a German general called 'that perfect thing apart' – the old British Regular Army that went to war in August 1914.

Old soldiers never die, they simply fade away. Memories also fade away with time but to those, now very few in number, who do remember, it must sometimes seem strange that the momentous events of the early months of the First World War now largely belong to history, and that the glory, if ever there was any, has departed.

It is a platitude to say that coming events cast their shadows before them, but in the case of World War I it is almost incredible how these events failed to impress Britain and the majority of her leaders until almost the last moment. The Army, though small, was at least prepared, thanks to the foresight of some of its generals. They were not listened to because the writing on the wall was either obliterated by events at home or by the calm induced by the prosperity of the Edwardian era.

When war did come the shock of a great European conflict was eased by the facile optimism of slogans such as 'over by Christmas' and 'business as usual'. It took the near-capture of Paris and the Channel ports, together with the casualty lists of autumn 1914, to shake the British Empire into an awareness of the true situation.

The role of the so-called 'Old Contemptibles' in saving Europe has been much under-estimated. It is true that German failures were perhaps more significant than Allied successes, but this book will try to put the part played by the British Army before the reader in its right perspective. What is really important is that the Retreat from Mons, followed by the Battle of the Marne and later by the First Battle of Ypres, deprived the Germans of their prime objectives and probably cost them the war. In helping to achieve this result the old Regular

Army, or that greater part of it which crossed to France in August 1914, practically ceased to exist.

It is inevitable that a comparison be made between the military operations at the beginning of both World Wars. Had the Germans captured their objectives, would the Allies have survived both the capture of Paris and the Channel ports? The French are highly sensitive to the loss of their capital and the British, forced to work on exterior lines, would have had to rely solely on the Royal Navy which, as Churchill said, could lose the war in an afternoon. Conversely, since the German Empire had failed in her main objectives, should she have realised that the war was lost and so tried to make peace?.

If either of these eventualities had materialised what would the future of Europe have been? The Kaiser's ambitions were limitless, as were Adolf Hitler's. Commercial jealousy is surely the root cause of great wars and had the Germans won in 1914 what would have been the price to be paid for their victory? If on the other hand they had given in, what exactions would the Allies have made? Another Versailles treaty and, later, the financial collapse of Germany would have been impossible after a negotiated peace, and thus a Second World War might have been avoided. The immediate result would surely have been to save millions of lives. These are all rhetorical questions and jobbing backwards is never a profitable occupation, but the fascination of the 'might have been' can perhaps excuse these very obvious objections.

In addition to the two chapters, one on the 'might have been' and the other on a comparison between the Retreat from Mons and the Retreat to Dunkirk, another has been added on the work of the infant Royal Flying Corps and the vital part it played in reporting enemy movements. It is true that the horse has always been an obsession of the military mind, but the early use of motor buses and rudimentary armoured cars showed what a vital part the internal combustion engine was to play in the future, a lesson often forgotten by parsimonious or apathetic governments.

In a book such as this it has been impossible to give in detail the part played by many of the lesser units. Most of these, notably the old Irish regiments, have long been disbanded. Many others are amalgamated to form composite units but have managed to retain some outward and visible sign of their old traditions. It is thought, however, that the history of one battalion which went through much of the campaign would be of interest, since the story of one is probably close to that of another. By a happy chance the 2nd Battalion The Essex Regiment fulfilled the necessary part. It is true that they were not at Mons but, coming out with the 4th Division, they arrived in time for the stand at Le Cateau and from then onwards fought through the period covered by this book.

The 2nd Essex, formerly the 56th Foot and known as the Pompadours, was raised in 1755 at the beginning of the Seven Years' War by Colonel Lord Charles Manners, a son of the Duke of Rutland. The men were recruited largely from the Newcastle-on-Tyne district. Legend has it that when, in 1764, the Colonel was refused the title of 'Royal' for the Regiment and the consequent wearing of blue facings, he chose purple, that being the favourite colour of Madame de Pompadour, the mistress of Louis XV of France. Presumably a second best.

When in 1881 the 56th Foot became the 2nd Battalion The Essex Regiment under the Childers reforms, there was great outcry when purple had to be changed to white as laid down for all non-Royal line regiments. Purple was not restored until 1936 when it was adopted by both battalions. Today the Essex forms part of the 3rd Royal Anglian Regiment, Pompadour still being preserved in a company title.

The part played by the Indian regiments in the First Battle of Ypres must also be remembered. What those unfortunate men had to suffer from the climate and from a full-scale European war, so utterly different from anything that some of them had experienced on the NW Frontier, or could possibly imagine, only emphasises their fortitude in a struggle whose causes could have meant little or nothing to them.

Forty Days in 1914 by Sir Frederick Maurice (Constable & Co. 1918), although written even before the end of the war but revised in 1920, still remains a classic and has been used freely. John Terraine, the acknowledged expert on the period, has been a very present help in trouble, and the late Sir Basil Liddell Hart, although not always acceptable to some, has had, right or wrong, probably more influence on the military thought of both World Wars than anyone else.

To name all the authorities used in the writing of this book would be tedious for the reader. A list of references is of course included in its proper place.

On a purely personal note my very best thanks are due for the great help given by my publishers Toby Buchan and Dominique Enright and their editor Randal Gray, who have borne with much fortitude the errors and omissions of a struggling author. Much help has been given by my friends at the National Army Museum and warm thanks are due to the Director, William Reid, for permission to publish the photographs and also to reproduce the picture which forms the dustjacket of this book.

The Reading Room of the Imperial War Museum has proved a considerable source of information for which I am very grateful, as I am to Roddy Suddaby of that museum for his help and advice in the early stages.

With regard to the part played by the 2nd Battalion The Essex Regiment in the period covered by this book, I am grateful to John H. Burrows & Sons Ltd. of Basildon for permission to quote *ad lib* from John William Burrows' *History of the Essex Regiment,* first published in 1927 by arrangement with the Essex Territorial Army Association.

I

OVERTURE AND BEGINNERS
1871-1914

> I was playing golf the day
> That the Germans landed;
> All our troops had run away,
> All our ships were stranded;
> And the thought of England's shame
> Altogether spoilt my game.

'The Englishman's home', *Harry Graham*

It is reported that Field-Marshal Graf Helmuth Karl von Moltke, the military architect of the German defeat of France in 1870-71, only smiled twice in his life: once when he was told that a French fortress was impregnable; and again when informed that his mother-in-law was dead.

Von Moltke died in 1891 but he had already appreciated that a new situation had arisen with regard to France. It was due first to the reorganisation of the French Army, second to her remarkably rapid economic recovery, in spite of the vast reparations demanded, and third, to the outspoken desire of all Frenchmen for revenge. There was also a Franco-Russian alliance to be taken into consideration that would entail a war on two fronts. Von Moltke's plan was first to defeat Russia and then to turn against France.

The nephew of this remarkable man, Colonel-General Helmuth Johannes von Moltke, who became Chief of the General Staff early in 1906, was to do exactly the reverse and so perhaps lose the war for Germany. The plan admittedly was not of his own choosing but was inherited from a predecessor, Graf Alfred von Schlieffen, but as will be seen later the alterations to this plan dictated by fresh circumstances were both military and political.

Von Moltke was the victim of his own defects, which will be considered in their proper place. Dismissed by the Kaiser in September 1914 he died in 1916, but not before he had called the old British Army 'that perfect thing apart' which,considering it was the chief instrument of his downfall,was indeed generous.

After the war of 1870-71 the Chancellor of a united German Empire, Prince Otto von Bismarck, wished to see his country the dominant power in Europe but with few colonial responsibilities. In this desire, which he held most strongly, he ran contrary to his young master Kaiser William II. The Kaiser wished for colonies. He had come badly out of the 'Scramble for Africa' compared with the British. He was jealous of the Royal Navy but above all he disliked his Uncle Bertie, the future Edward VII, whom he felt patronised him. The dislike was mutual and the antagonists were only kept apart by Queen Victoria who, towards the end of her long reign, had to exercise all her authority as grandmother of Europe.

The differences of opinion between the Kaiser and Bismarck resulted in the resignation of the Chancellor in 1890, which far-reaching event was immortalised in the famous *Punch* cartoon 'Dropping the Pilot'.

Combined with the Kaiser's somewhat ludicrous goings-on in the Near East and North Africa, which will be referred to later in the chapter, there was a more serious threat to European peace posed by German overtures to the newly arisen Young Turk Party under their leader Enver Pasha. The consequent construction of the Berlin-Baghdad Railway could not be ignored by either Britain or France, since their spheres of influence in Egypt and the Levant were threatened.

If these problems were not enough,there were perhaps even greater ones in Central Europe. The defeat of Austria by Prussia at Sadowa in 1866 had forced Austria into the German camp. The Hapsburg Austro-Hungarian Empire under the aged Emperor Francis Joseph was tottering due to her internal ethniç problems and was at loggerheads with Russia, which felt herself to be the champion of all Orthodox Christians in the Balkans.

It only needed a spark to ignite the fuel,and this was provided by the assassination, on 28 June 1914, of the Hapsburg heir to the Austrian throne, Archduke Francis Ferdinand, at Sarajevo in Bosnia, by a Serbian student called Princip.

Before Sarajevo, in spite of outpourings both literary and dramatic, little impact was made on a British general public more concerned with the pleasures of Edwardian peace than with the possibilities of a

14

war with a supposedly friendly continental power. There were, however, graver and more persistent warnings. *The Riddle of the Sands* by Erskine Childers told in the form of a novel how two yachtsmen discovered massive German preparations among the Frisian Islands for an invasion of Britain across the North Sea. This 1903 book made a considerable impression on the more thinking members of the public. It is said that Winston Churchill stayed up all night reading it (this nocturnal eccentricity would, however, be completely in character). There were, however, greater movements afoot mightier than the pen.

The attitude of Germany before and during the Boer War in South Africa (1899-1902) had been anything but friendly. The Kaiser had sent a notorious telegram to President Kruger congratulating him on the collapse of the ill-starred Jameson Raid in 1896. The Kaiser's subsequent junketings and the general tone of his speeches had hardly allayed the fears of more far-seeing British politicians and a small number of the less-inhibited Service chiefs. The Army, however, was still being trained for colonial service even though great improvements had been made in firepower following the lessons learned in South Africa.

Field-Marshal Lord Roberts had taken over command in South Africa in succession to General Sir Redvers Buller following the disasters of 'Black Week' in December 1899. Roberts's claim to fame had been a long and successful career in India which included the famous march through Afghanistan from Kabul to Kandahar in 1880. Prior to that march there had been two well-executed turning movements in Afghanistan, which proved their worth against an enemy fearful for his communications. A similar but wider movement against the Boers had proved equally successful and had resulted in the capture of Pretoria, the capital city. Roberts returned home in triumph after this victory which, however, did not end the war. It was left to General Sir Herbert Kitchener to bring the whole sorry business to a close. The turning movement had nevertheless considerably impressed the Germans, who had such a movement on a far-larger scale very much in mind, but with Europe as the battlefield.

Roberts had succeeded Field-Marshal Lord Wolseley as Commander-in-Chief in 1901, but in 1904, as a result of the report of Lord Esher's Committee, a general staff was created with a chief whose title was eventually to be Chief of the Imperial General Staff or, succinctly, CIGS. In this way the historic post of Commander-in-Chief was abolished and Roberts was somewhat ignominiously retired.

In 1902 Roberts, accompanied by Lieutenant-General Sir John French, who had commanded the cavalry in South Africa, attended the German Army manoeuvres. They were impressed by the staffwork and organisation shown but not by the tactics, which consisted largely of attacks carried out in mass formation. They came to the conclusion that these would be 'damnably mauled', as Wellington would have said, which was to be proved in the early months of 1914.

After his retirement Roberts began a crusade for national service (a form of conscription), convinced as he was of a German threat. With a few devoted adherents he stumped the country preaching the menace of Prussian militarism. People flocked to his meetings not to hear bad news but to see little 'Bobs', the hero of the hour. Eventually the middle class did pay some attention, fearing for their prosperity, but with the Establishment he was highly unpopular and made little or no impact on the governments of the day which feared for their majorities. What at this time then was the Army's attitude to a German war? The answer lay in ever-closer links with France.

At the turn of the century Franco-British relations were at a low ebb. The attitude of France during the Boer War was on a par with Germany's. There was, however, soon to be a rapid change. In June 1902 the Triple Alliance of 1881 was renewed between Germany, Austria–Hungary and Italy. France felt herself isolated in Western Europe since Russia was her only ally (by 1894 treaty) and of doubtful value. In April 1904 King Edward VII's influence behind the scenes did much to help the formation of an Entente Cordiale following a visit to London the previous year by President Loubet and his Foreign Minister, Théophile Delcassé. A Conservative Government with Arthur Balfour as Prime Minister was in office. This Entente could in no way be considered as a definite alliance, but, in view of Russia's defeat by Japan in 1905 and the Kaiser's very evident colonial ambitions, France was in great need of a friend close at hand able and willing to give her military support.

As has been seen, great reorganisation had taken place at the War Office in 1904. An important feature of this reorganisation was the creation of a Directorate of Military Operations. The first Director was Major-General James Grierson, who had been Military Attaché in

Berlin and who was well aware of the German menace.

By December 1905 a Liberal Government was in office under Sir Henry Campbell-Bannerman, and the French rather naturally were anxious to know what its attitude would be regarding military support. Later in the month Colonel Victor Huguet, the French Military Attaché in London, tried to sound out Grierson on the situation. It is at this point that a certain Colonel Charles Repington, who had left the army due to a divorce scandal and was at this time Military Correspondent of *The Times*, acted as a go-between for Grierson and Sir Edward Grey, the Foreign Secretary. The result was that Grey gave his support to the policy of the previous government. Early in 1906 Paul Cambon, the French Ambassador in London, had a consultation with Sir Edward Grey. No formal alliance was suggested, but the French wished to know whether, if attacked by Germany, Britain would come to their aid. The whole question was then referred by Grey to the Committee of Imperial Defence and joint military planning was agreed.

As a result Grierson began to make arrangements with Huguet for the landing of a British force in France. Grierson, with Lieutenant-Colonel William Robertson as his staff officer, reconnoitred the Franco-Belgian frontier with a view to choosing concentration areas and lines of advance and communication.

In his autobiography, *From Private to Field-Marshal*, Robertson wrote:

> In combination with Colonel Huguet, Grierson did more than any other officer of his time to establish good relations between the French and British armies, and it is true to say that the success which attended the dispatch of the British Expeditionary Force in 1914 was due first and foremost to his initiative and foresight when he was Director of Military Operations in 1904-06.

Due largely to the easing of tension over Morocco between France and Germany as a result of the Algeçiras Conference, and a new Director of Military Operations less dynamic than Grierson, nothing further transpired for another four years, that is to say until August 1910.

There now appears on the scene a character who, in spite of what Sir William Robertson said, probably did far more than Grierson to foster good relations with the French. Henry Wilson had failed for both

17

Woolwich and Sandhurst military academies on numerous occasions. One is reminded of the old story of the Sandhurst entrant, who when asked how much string it would take to measure up the various spans of a bridge, wrote 'balls and balls like the rest of the other bloody questions' and walked out. The candidate probably got into the cavalry in much the same way that Wilson got into the Rifle Brigade – through the Irish Militia.

Henry Wilson was an Ulsterman of much shrewdness and charm, as well as a born intriguer. He also had the gift of speaking excellent French. Furthermore, he was an ardent disciple of Lord Roberts in all that the latter had tried to do regarding army reform and national service. By 1909 Wilson had become Commandant of the Staff College at the same time as Ferdinand Foch was Director of the *École Supérieure de Guerre*, the French equivalent. The two met on many occasions and Wilson fell much under the influence of Foch, but their friendship was of immense value in promoting and furthering understanding between the two armies.

In August 1910 Wilson became Director of Military Operations, and co-operation between the two armies became once more a live force. From this time onwards all Wilson's persuasive powers (and his genius for intrigue) were directed towards a real liaison with the French. Foch had convinced him, if he had needed convincing, of the German menace and this doctrine Wilson was able to communicate not only to the CIGS, General Sir William Nicholson, but also through him to Sir Edward Grey, the Foreign Secretary.

It must not be thought that Wilson's lack of ability to pass examinations detracted in any way from his professional skill; many distinguished persons have suffered from the same disability without serious disadvantage. He was a born soldier, although his penchant for intrigue marred his reputation. His life was tragically cut short at the hands of Irish assassins in 1922.

If further proof of Germany's intentions were needed, it was certainly provided by the events which followed. On 1 July 1911 the German gunboat *Panther* arrived at Agadir, on the Moroccan coast, in order, so it was stated, to protect German interests threatened by long-established French influence in that country. To the British, this action was as obnoxious as it was to the French, since Britain's sea supremacy would be menaced if, as it was supposed, Germany was bent on setting up a naval base on the Atlantic coast.

A famous Mansion House speech by David Lloyd George, the Chancellor of the Exchequer, put over with all the fire of which that mercurial Welshman was capable, induced the Germans, and more particularly the Kaiser, to understand the consequences should Britain become involved. They chose discretion and withdrew, thus delaying a European war for another three years.

As a result of the Agadir crisis, however, a written agreement was drawn up between France and Britain. Although not considered to be binding on either government, certain definite plans were made to determine the composition and the ports of disembarkation of the BEF, and also the day-to-day order of the arrival of British troops in France.

These plans, and the further consultations which took place up to the time of the declaration of war on 4 August 1914, did much to ensure the rapid and secret transport of the expeditionary force to its destination.

To Henry Wilson, therefore, must be given full credit for the vital part that he played in convincing not only the 'frocks', as he called the politicians, but also the military hierarchy, of the vital necessity for a co-ordinated plan between the two armies to meet the threat of a German attack on France and the Low Countries. Whether this plan was the right one will be considered later, but the actions that he did take would seem, in view of the circumstances at the time, to have been the only ones possible.

II

WAR PLANS 1891-1914

Sir Frederick Maurice, in his book *Forty Days in 1914*, wrote: 'When I landed at Havre on 11 August 1914 a French colonel who had come down to meet our party said to me "Now that the British Army is coming the result is certain. This time the Germans have bitten off more than they can chew"; and this represented the opinion of both armies at the time.'

He went on to say (and his words are quoted in full):

The news of the French invasion of Lorraine and of the stout resistance of Liège confirmed this view, and until the actual tidings of disaster arrived all seemed going well. It was then that the peoples of the Entente nations learned that the fortress of Namur had fallen in forty-eight hours and that the German armies were sweeping through Belgium and Northern France, everywhere in overwhelming numbers. It was with consternation that Great Britain heard the news for which she was completely unprepared, that her little army, all but surrounded, was as good as lost and that Paris lay at the mercy of the enemy. Then, still more amazing, came the later news that the Germans were in full retreat, that Paris was saved and that our men were advancing victoriously, taking prisoners and guns. How did our army escape? Why did not the Germans enter Paris, and why did they retreat?

In order to appreciate this remarkable turn of events it is first necessary to see how the German plans were laid, and then to consider what the French intended to do or not to do to counteract them, and what was to be the role of the British Army.

In 1891 Graf Alfred von Schlieffen became Chief of the General Staff in succession to the elder von Moltke. He was to take an entirely different view of the problem of which nation to attack first. The

Russians, it was argued, due to a natural slowness and the vastness of the country, would take a considerably greater time to mobilise than the French. It was therefore essential that the French be destroyed first and Russia dealt with later.

It is easy to see that one of the reasons for German fears was the reorganisation of the French Army after the disastrous war of 1870-71. But what was to influence German strategic thinking far more was the French plan of defence. After the defeat in 1870-71 Alsace and Lorraine were incorporated into the new German confederation. The Rhine was no longer the national frontier. In consequence a chain of fortifications was constructed along the whole length of the common frontier with only one gap, the Trouée des Charmes, about fifty miles wide, between the two fortresses of Toul and Epinal. Behind this natural feature the French field army would be massed. These frontier defences could only be outflanked by a movement south through Switzerland, a country notoriously difficult in which to manoeuvre; or north through Luxembourg and Belgium, the neutrality of which had been guaranteed by the Great Powers, including Germany, by treaties in 1839 and 1871.

The Schlieffen Plan, completed in 1905, ordained a great right-wing sweep through Belgium in order to take Paris from the west and so pin the French armies against their eastern defences from the rear. For this vast enterprise five armies would be necessary, while only two would contain the main French Army concentrated for a thrust to regain the lost provinces. The plan had two major flaws: the possible lack of enough first-line divisions for such an undertaking, and the likelihood of a counter-attack in the flank to which any turning movement is obviously subject.

'Keep the right strong' besought Schlieffen on his deathbed in 1913. In his own vivid phraseology 'the last grenadier on the right wing should brush the Channel with his sleeve'. Early in 1906 he had been succeeded by the younger von Moltke, a man of very different temperament and ability from his uncle. Originally only ten divisions had been assigned to the Russian front. By the time the after-effects of Russia's defeat by Japan had been overcome von Moltke found it necessary to detach another four divisions to hold the Russians in check.

Von Moltke was not the man his uncle had been. He was more of a charming courtier to his master the Kaiser than the possessor of enough belligerence to carry out a plan of such vast conception. What he in fact did was to weaken the right wing and so deprive the plan of its main object, that of complete envelopment, for fear of a possible French penetration into Lorraine.

What then were the French plans following the reorganisation of their army? There were in fact no fewer than seventeen of these devised between 1875 and 1914, mainly influenced in their design by motives of regaining the lost provinces and the possible lines of advance open to them.

French military thinking was still governed by memories of the great Napoleon; Waterloo had perhaps been conveniently forgotten. France did not in fact possess a leader equal even to a Marshal of the Empire whereas their opponents did not suffer from the defects of Napoleon's Prussian contemporaries. Under the guidance of successive commanders and directors of the *École Supérieure de Guerre,* an insistence on the offensive was indoctrinated into all ranks. This brainwashing was necessary not only to rebuild morale but also to carry a war into German-held territory as quickly as possible.

Russia was an ally, and if British help was assured some parity could be counted on between the field armies of France and Germany, if the longer period of French military service was also taken into consideration.

The defection of a German staff officer as early as 1904 disclosed to the French the basis of the Schlieffen Plan. This vital information seems to have had little or no effect on their high command. Only a very few senior officers took it seriously, most suspecting that Germany would not dare to concentrate so great a proportion of her strength on the Western Front.

Unlike the Germans, who were cynically prepared to disregard the neutrality of Belgium, the French planners were limited to a direct assault across the frontier. The subsequent French invasion of Alsace-Lorraine was not only dictated by motives of revenge, but also by the limitations of the terrain if an invasion through Belgium was discounted on moral grounds.

By 1914 Plan XVII had been drawn up, mercifully the final one of the series. It is almost beyond belief that it ignored all the information that the French intelligence service must have amassed regarding German intentions. The plan blandly assumed that the major part of the German Army would be concentrated on the frontier and that the French would attack them there with all their forces.

It must be remembered that among those few senior officers mentioned above were Foch and his British admirer, Henry Wilson. But where did the British Army come into all this? In so far as Plan XVII was concerned the answer was nowhere. In spite of all the planning by Grierson and Wilson, there is no reference anywhere in it to a participation by the British.

In 1910 General Victor Michel was appointed Vice-President of the *Conseil Supérieur de la Guerre*; in the event of war he would command the field army. Michel was another of the few senior officers who believed that the Germans were determined on a right flanking movement through Belgium, and his plan was one of defence along the whole frontier. The British were actually mentioned, although in a reserve capacity. The plan was sensible and would have avoided falling into the Schlieffen trap. It was execrated by the attack-at-all-costs school, and also came under pressure from commercial interests such as the Forges de France, and since these wild men had the ear of Adolphe Messimy, the War Minister, Michel had to go. He was succeeded by General Joseph Jacques Césaire Joffre. 'Papa' Joffre was the complete opposite of the average Englishman's idea of a Frenchman. He was large, stolid and unflappable, qualities which were to stand him in good stead later.

Foch himself had by this time (1910) become convinced of the German right flank threat, and he tried to influence Joffre through his military assistant, a certain Commandant Maurice Gamelin, later to become well known as the Commander-in-Chief of the French Army at the beginning of the Second World War. Foch also laid great stress on his collaboration with Wilson, and Joffre was so impressed that he now considered the role of the Expeditionary Force to be a prolongation of the French left flank, thus helping to spearhead a possible counter-attack against a too-extended German right.

The role of the BEF also depended upon the actual situation in Britain. As has been seen, many reforms in the administration of the Army had taken place due to the recommendations of the Esher Committee. In 1906 a Liberal Government had come into power. Military problems or reforms on a large scale have never been noticeably a Liberal Party heritage, and this government followed the usual pattern of mild pacifism. Liberal Secretaries of State for War do seem, however, to be glaring exceptions to the usual run of Liberal politicians, as exemplified by Edward Cardwell and Hugh Childers under Gladstone, and then by Richard Haldane under Campbell-Bannerman and, later, Asquith.

Lord Haldane, as he subsequently became, was perhaps the greatest war minister that this country has produced. He realized that to fight in Europe as the ally of France was essential if Germany was to be frustrated in her plans for European domination. It was for this reason that the BEF was reorganised into a coherent fighting force of two army corps, comprising three divisions each and a cavalry division. Haldane was also responsible for the creation of a Territorial Force to replace the old Volunteers, recruited not only for home defence but also to act as a reserve standby for the Regular Army on an individual volunteer basis. Just as Wolseley had been the *eminence grise* of Cardwell and Childers, it hardly needs to be said that this function was ably filled for Haldane by that wily operator Henry Wilson.

To cut out the frills, the basic plan was for the British Army to assemble round Maubeuge and act on the left flank of the French. This plan became the sacred cow of Wilson, and in default of any other it dominated all the plans for mobilisation and safe transport of the BEF to France. Like so much of the planning on both sides, it proved abortive through strategic and personal misconceptions, misunderstandings and mistrust.

III

DRAMATIS PERSONAE AUGUST 1914

Lieutenant-General Sir Douglas Haig, who was to command I Corps of the BEF in the early part of the war and later succeeded Sir John French as Commander-in-Chief in France, was one of those generals who have real difficulty in ingratiating themselves with the lower ranks of the army. This lack of communication has been shared by some but not noticeably by others. Which of the two kinds are the better commanders it is not easy to decide.

Eventually Haig, it is said, was persuaded by his staff that some effort had to be made to remedy this defect. He therefore set out, accompanied by a glittering escort, to try and see what he could do about it. As all this took place well behind the lines he shortly came across one of the ancillary units. Selecting probably the dirtiest soldier in the whole BEF, Haig said in somewhat staccato tones 'And where did you start this war, my man?' The unfortunate individual, so overawed by these momentous words, answered 'Gor blimey, Governor [or words to that effect], I didn't start it.'

This sentiment would also seem to sum up pretty well the attitude of the average old regular. 'We're here because we're here', and it didn't matter very much if the enemy were French or German, they were all foreigners anyway. There was a job to be done and they were there to do it. Bitterness and enmity tended to exist between 1st and 2nd Battalions or between those regiments which were traditionally hostile to each other for some long-forgotten reason.

There might also have been considerable resentment among some troops. It must be remembered that the home battalions were used as feeders for those on foreign service and so were considerably under strength. As a result the Expeditionary Force contained a high proportion of reservists, as high as seventy per cent in some units, who had been hastily recalled to the colours; many of them had good jobs and were happily settled down with wives and families. To these men the war must have come as a bitter blow, but to others not so fortunate it was heaven-sent.

War to the regular officer of the period had one great advantage in that it offered distinct possibilities of long-overdue promotion. It did, however, interfere with the hunting season and other social distractions then considered of great importance.

In spite of appearances it must never be thought that the British Army at this time was not an exceedingly efficient and highly trained fighting force. It was small, of course, but the idea that it was unprepared for war is entirely false. The country *was* unprepared, but the Army, as is witnessed by the speed of its mobilisation and transportation to France, was ready and, to a great extent, willing.

Professionalism among all ranks was of the highest order. Von Moltke's 'perfect thing apart' was not yet contaminated (as the professionals would have thought) by the enthusiastic amateur. Swords were sent to be sharpened. Their owners neither thought that they would, in so short a time, be beaten into toasting forks in the muddy trenches of the Aisne, nor that within three months they themselves would have become virtually extinct.

'One by one', said Sir Edward Grey, the Foreign Secretary, 'the lamps are going out all over Europe.' The first of these lights, and perhaps the most unscrupulous extinction, went out on 28 July 1914, when Austria declared war on the unfortunate Serbia, held responsible for the murder of the Archduke Francis Ferdinand. This declaration automatically included that of Germany. Russia and her ally France were quickly involved, on 1 and 3 August respectively. But while France immediately responded in kind, Britain, due largely to Liberal Government misgivings, delayed until midnight on 4 August, much to French annoyance since any parity in mobilisation would be upset. It was only pious horror at the German violation of Belgium's neutrality that turned the scale. On the face of it, this reason seems to be the merest hypocrisy. Military Intelligence must surely have informed the Government of at least the likelihood of such a move by Germany, but governments have to consider their majorities, and the Liberals of that time the non-conformist vote especially.

Major-General J. F. C. Fuller in his book *The Conduct of War*

26

1789-1961 says: 'In addition the Treaty of 1839, which guaranteed the neutrality of Belgium, British obligations were not defined nor was there any provision which necessitated England sending troops to Belgium to make war on any power that should violate her territories.'

The Liberals need not have worried – the country went wild with joy. The British, or more correctly perhaps, the English, are extraordinary in their mass emotions. They are capable not only of the most ridiculous enthusiasms and unrighteous indignation, but also of a dour endurance in times of real trouble. It was the civilian population which rather naturally showed the greatest outward desire for war since, at the outset anyway, they did not have to go to it – bombardment from the air was a horror of the future.

The spy scares; the hounding out of office of men such as Haldane and Prince Louis of Battenberg (the First Sea Lord) for supposed German sympathies; the white feathers; and the 'We don't want to lose you but we think you ought to go' type of song were all symptoms of an hysteria which was accompanied by the equally unpleasant slogan of 'business as usual'.

War then had come. It is therefore now essential to take stock of those personalities who will shape the course of events during the dramatic months to follow.

It was said that at the outbreak of war it was only Asquith, the Prime Minister, and Kitchener, who had on 5 August become War Minister, who realised that it was going to be a long drawn-out affair. 'Over by Christmas' was the almost universal opinion, both civilian and military.

Of Asquith much has been written. Little need be said here, except perhaps that he was a high security risk due to his letters on affairs of state to his soulmate, Lady Venetia Stanley, and also to the verbal indiscretions of his redoubtable wife Margot.

Kitchener is one of the more remarkable figures of history. A legend in his lifetime, he was perhaps lucky, in terms of his reputation, to die when he did, in June 1916, when the cruiser HMS *Hampshire* struck a U-boat mine off the Orkneys as the 'War Lord', as he had become, was on his way to Russia. It has often been said that his time had run out. He had suffered much criticism in the Northcliffe press (*The Times* and *Daily Mail*) and in many ways had become an embarrassment to his colleagues, although he still remained the idol of the people and of the Army he had created.

As Sir Philip Magnus says in his excellent biography: 'The masses acclaimed Kitchener as a man of action. He was no tactician, was useless for team work and thus no administrator. He was a strange mixture of hardness and kindness.' Again to quote Magnus,'His two basic attributes were an unparalleled thoroughness and an unparalleled drive.' He was incapable of delegation and until his death he ran World War I, not only creating an Army called after him, but dominating the rest of the Cabinet by the force of his personality.

Kitchener, a Royal Engineer, was not mad, married or Methodist, as all sappers were supposed to be. He was, however, certainly different. All his service had been overseas and he was completely ignorant of how a modern army was run. As has been said above he had no tactical ability. His victory at Omdurman, against the Dervishes in the Sudan in 1898, was mainly the result of a timely maneouvre by Major-General Sir Hector Macdonald's brigade.

Kitchener, sixty-four in 1914, was incapable of delegation and relied entirely on his great powers of intuition, improvisation, and a force of character which inspired terror into lesser mortals. He was obviously to play a vital part in the events to follow, more especially in his dealings with Sir John French, the sixty-two year-old Commander-in-Chief of the BEF.

As the campaign develops so will the character of that highly controversial figure 'Johnny French'. John Denton Pinkstone French had shown great talent as a cavalry general in the Boer War. He was of the *arme blanche* school as characterised in Walter Scott's lines, ' "Charge, Chester, charge, On, Stanley on," Were the last words of Marmion.' Similar orders were to be the last words of many others not so immortalised, but such a 'cavalry spirit' was to persist, long after mechanisation, into the Western Desert. It was always anathema to Wellington and later led Roberts and many other senior officers to subscribe to a more dismounted role for cavalry.

French, to give him his due, also realised the importance of training the cavalry to use with effect the Lee-Enfield .303 standard infantry pattern rifle. Efficiency with the rifle in mounted units was to pay high dividends in the battles to come. History has done scant justice to French, preferring instead to dwell on his failures rather than on his good qualities. Unfortunately for those concerned, this is the way of history written almost exclusively by enemies or rivals and, in this case, by French's own *1914*, which is full of inconsistencies and inaccuracies.

The son of a sailor (both parents died young), French was brought up by a somewhat odd collection of older sisters and destined for the Navy, in which he reached the rank of midshipman. Feeling that this service was not for him since he loved horses and loathed heights he, like others mentioned, entered the Army through the militia. His regiment, the 19th Hussars, was not quite so 'smart' and consequently less expensive than some others, which was probably just as well.

Unlike many cavalry officers of the day, he took a keen interest in his profession and this eccentricity, combined with fortunate contacts due to his charm of manner, ensured rapid promotion. The steps which led him to become CIGS by 1911, were slippery indeed, due to an inability to handle money and also to a marked aptitude for seduction.

His abilities had led him, despite his faults, to the top of his profession but in March 1914 a blow was to hit the Army right below the belt. This most unfortunate event for all concerned was known as the Curragh 'Incident' or even 'Mutiny'. The Curragh camp was the Aldershot of Ireland, a centre of military activity outside Dublin.

The situation in Ulster has now, even with its attendant horrors, become almost a commonplace. So used are the public in England to the problems created by ceaseless terrorism that, with the exception of some particularly revolting crime, they pass almost without comment. It would be pointless to go back in history to Cromwell or the Battle of the Boyne. The more modern problems of potato famine, the Fenians and absentee landlords, if not forgotten in Ireland, are more remembered in the United States where, as someone has said, 'Government by the Irish for the Jews shall not perish from the earth'. (This is to parody Lincoln at Gettysburg; who also in his turn got the true version from Charles Wesley.)

To us now the Easter Rising of 1916, the 'troubles' of 1921, and the subsequent treaty are the events of a past age 'old unhappy far-off things and battles long ago'. It seems almost incredible, therefore, in view of the present situation, that in the early spring of 1914 ball ammunition was issued to the British troops stationed at the Curragh in order to coerce Ulster into becoming part of a united Ireland.

Gladstone had attempted some form of Home Rule without success and now Asquith's Liberal Government was determined to give Home Rule to Ireland as a whole. To the South, Catholic and undeveloped, this was manna from heaven, but to the North, fiercely Protestant, industrialised and largely Scots by origin, it was a gross betrayal of all they held dear.

Two men, John Redmond in the South and Sir Edward Carson in the North, were the dynamic forces behind the two factions. Public sympathy in the rest of Britain was definitely with the North, where Carson had rallied 80,000 armed volunteers with the slogan 'Ulster will fight and Ulster will be right'. It is not surprising, in view of the situation today, that at that time both sides were prepared to go to war. What is surprising is that the Government was prepared to use the Army to coerce the North.

The situation within the Army was problematic. It seems never to have occurred to the Government that a high proportion not only of officers but also of NCOs and men serving were of Irish extraction. Although men from both the North and South seem to serve happily together in British regiments, as in the Irish Guards today, only a politician would expect them to shoot at their fellow countrymen.

It is not surprising that the two officers most concerned in the affair, Roberts, the senior officer in the Army (a field-marshal never retires), and Brigadier-General Hubert Gough, commanding the cavalry brigade at the Curragh, should be the most vehement and active in their determination that regular soldiers should not be used against Ulster. Oddly enough, both men were from the South.

The whole situation was grossly mishandled by Colonel John Seely, the War Minister, and by General Sir Arthur Paget, who was the C-in-C in Ireland. So confused were the orders or instructions issued by these two that the various senior officers concerned literally did not know if they were coming or going. Gough took the most definite line of all, threatening to send in his papers should the Army be used to coerce Ulster, and carrying with him the majority of the officers not only at the Curragh but in England also. Gough was relieved of his command and threatened with court martial. This threat was in itself absurd, since there was no reference in the *Manual of Military Law* to cover such an action in the event of a *civil* war.

Roberts had a first-class row with Seely and cut French in the street. French did not like Roberts anyway which, although beside the point, obviously did nothing to help so delicate a situation. The fairest thing that can be said about French was that he sat on the fence perching very much on that part which leant towards the Government. He feared that if he did not do so he would lose the command of the BEF in the event of war.

King George V smoothed matters over to a certain extent and Asquith,the 'wait and see' expert,temporised or,as George Robey sang, 'Mr Asquith said in a voice sweet and calm, another little drink wouldn't do us any harm.' Fortunately Haldane, the one man of sense, eventually declared that force would never be used against Ulster.

It is surprising how pacifists act when they are not asked to go to war themselves. Viscount Morley, who held up pious hands of horror against war with Germany, was quite prepared in Cabinet to allow military force to be used against his own countrymen. Winston Churchill also, hardly a pacifist, added fuel to the fire by a speech at Bradford; he was of course ever a politician. This sorry business was completely overshadowed by the events which followed,but the story has been told at some length because of the influence the Curragh Incident had on French. The Army made a rapid recovery, but French did not.

Since the Government had climbed down and the CIGS had sided with it,French was obliged to resign. To a man of his temperament this was a staggering blow. His financial affairs were at their lowest ebb. His friends found him plunged in gloom, as it would seem that his resignation had put paid to his chances of commanding the BEF in the event of war. He was not to remain long in this mood of despair, however. His abilities had not been forgotten and the job was still his.

Of Irish extraction, French was squat, hot-tempered, prone to extremes of depression and elation but, like Roberts and Buller, was among the few generals who, under all circumstances, held the affection of the private soldier. It has already been said that he got to the top by a combination of his own ability, and also by his capacity to charm the right people at the right time.

Unfortunately this charm did not extend to his two corps commanders, Sir Douglas Haig and Sir Horace Smith-Dorrien. Originally Lieutenant-General Sir James Grierson, possible the ablest officer in the Army, had been chosen as the commander of II Corps, but tragically he had died from a heart attack in a train on the way to take up his appointment. Much to French's disgust he had had the fifty-six-year-old Smith-Dorrien thrust on him by Kitchener. It is perhaps idle to speculate what would have happened if Grierson had lived. He spoke both German and French fluently. Would he have been, in 1915, a far more imaginative successor to Sir John than Haig?

Grierson's death was a personal grief to both French and Haig. The immediate consequences, had he survived, would have been that relations would have been far better, not only between GHQ and II Corps but also those between the two individual corps commanders. As it was, in each instance they could hardly have been much worse.

Douglas Haig, the 'Educated Soldier' as John Terraine calls him, was the fifty-three-year-old product of Clifton, Brasenose College, Oxford and the 7th Hussars, a 'smarter' cavalry regiment than the 19th. He had been French's brigade major both in peace and in South Africa, and had shared much of the glory. For a long time they were good friends. Haig, a member of the whisky family, was a rich man, French was not, largely due to his way of life. At a particularly low ebb in his finances French had borrowed a large sum of money from Haig which had never been repaid (and never was).

The propriety of such a transaction between senior and junior is obviously open to doubt, and it certainly soured the relations between the two men. As a result of his loss of trust between them Haig began to have grave doubts as to Sir John's capacity for high command.

Both Haig and Smith-Dorrien had a direct line to the King, which must have been very galling to the C-in-C since they could both criticise their chief to the monarch, which obviously put French in an exceedingly awkward situation. In talking to the King, Haig had said about French: 'I had grave doubts, however, whether his temper was sufficiently even or his military knowledge sufficiently thorough to enable him to discharge properly the very difficult duties which will devolve upon him. In my own heart I know that French is quite unfit for this great command in time of crisis.' Hardly a good beginning.

Lieutenant-General Sir Horace Smith-Dorrien had served for long with distinction in the colonial wars. From Harrow he had entered the 45th Regiment (later the Sherwood Foresters) as early as 1876, and was one of the few survivors of Isandhlwana in the Zulu War of 1879. It appears that since he was wearing blue patrols and not a red

32

coat he was thought to be a civilian, which says much for the sensibilities of the Zulus.

That he was an infantryman and a supporter, like Wilson, of Roberts and the anti-*arme blanche* school, was probably not of great importance with regard to the animosity between him and French. What had soured their relations was that when Smith-Dorrien became GOC at Aldershot in succession to French he had instituted many reforms for the benefit of the troops, and irksome regulations which had been disliked were abolished.

French, although so popular, was a strong disciplinarian and he felt that what Smith-Dorrien had done reflected adversely on his time as GOC. The last straw as far as French was concerned was that his successor criticised the cavalry for their indifferent musketry. Smith-Dorrien, although popular with the troops, had a violent temper which reduced the victims of his wrath to pulp. This lack of balance had prevented him being chosen as C-in-C in India. But as early as 1912 Smith-Dorrien had been posted as the commander of II Corps with Grierson as chief of staff, so there was some precedent for Kitchener's choice, unfortunate though it was.

Of the fifty-year-old Major-General Henry Wilson much has already been said. He was to be French's strength and stay as Deputy Chief of Staff, upholding an extremely shaky creation unlike Lieutenant-General Sir Archibald Murray who, although Chief of Staff, was to become more and more of a passenger due to his holding a position that was beyond his capacity.

The situation was a gloomy one, and fraught with danger. A chief at variance, to put it mildly, with his two subordinate commanders; the senior staff officer largely incompetent; and the C-in-C himself mistrustful of the Secretary of State, and of uncertain temperament. It would seem that the court jester, Wilson, would be running the show. Little hope then for the success of the play – a miracle would be needed to keep it going.

IV

BEF MOBILISATION AND ADVANCE 5-21 AUGUST

The prelude to the things to come was about to take shape, a shape shadowy rather than substantial. On the afternoon of 5 August 1914 a strange collection of 'frocks' and generals assembled at 10 Downing Street to discuss what was to be done. The French frontier fortress of Maubeuge, as had been already planned by the War Office, was designated as the BEF concentration area. The 'War Office' was in effect Wilson in collaboration with his French friends. Speed was essential in the dispatch of the army to France, due to British mobilisation being so much behind that of the French.

Sir John French, having duly emphasised this point, went off at a tangent and, to the apparent dismay of the military, suggested that Antwerp might be a better choice since from this Belgian fortress and port city a flank attack could be launched against the German right. This last-minute change of mind is somewhat similar, though on a much smaller scale, to the Kaiser's *volte face*, when at the outbreak of war, in a premature assumption that England would remain neutral, he proposed to von Moltke that the Schlieffen Plan should be changed and Russia attacked first. Although this imperial bombshell created a far greater explosion than did the Antwerp idea, both served to emphasise the impossibility of a change of plan once mobilisation has begun.

The Antwerp plan was quashed by Winston Churchill which, in view of coming events, seems strange, to say the least of it. The First Lord of the Admiralty decided that the safety of the longer sea-crossing could not be guaranteed by the Royal Navy. Several voices were raised in suggesting that Amiens was a safer concentration area than Maubeuge, Kitchener and Churchill being among the more prominent. The veteran Lord Roberts also favoured an area farther back. In the end, however, Maubeuge was agreed upon as being the only possible assembly area in view of the plans already made.

During the next few days many wrangles took place and many questions were left unanswered. The most obvious was the problem of how invasion was to be met and consequently what reserve it was necessary to keep in England. Kitchener and French were at once at loggerheads over the number of troops to be left at home, Kitchener taking the view that the war would be long and French the opposite.

'K' and Wilson then had a row over the fact that Colonel Huguet, acting as French liaison officer between the two armies, had not paid his respects to the new War Minister and had also gone off with the British mobilisation plans in his pocket. Sir John French therefore gained an ally in Wilson, which boded ill for his future relations with Kitchener, which were already very strained.

A further meeting between 'K' and Wilson, this time with Huguet and other French officers, took place on 12 August. After a long and heated discussion, which drove Wilson to distraction, Kitchener's fears of a concentration too far forward were overcome; admittedly, no mean feat on Wilson's part. Time and time again, Wilson's Figaro-like character swayed more prudent judgements.

Kitchener, neither strategist nor tactician, and with little knowledge of Continental armies except that gained as a twenty-year-old volunteer ambulance driver with the French in 1871, relied solely on his intuition. This sixth sense warned against the BEF falling into a trap. Wilson, infatuated with the French connection and the attack-at-all-costs school of thought, could not or would not see the dangers. It was Kitchener the 'ignoramus' who was right; what a pity it was that he did not exercise his vast powers in this vital choice rather than in others of far less merit.

The reason given for Kitchener's mistrust of the Territorial Force created by Haldane seems almost incredible. It is said that he had seen the French Territorials in action during the Franco-Prussian War and, influenced by their bad showing, assumed that British Territorials were in the same category as a gaggle of elderly reservists.

The Territorial Force had home defence as its primary role, and that admittedly was its only liability. The great majority of its members had, however, volunteered for foreign service. Consequently through the County Associations the Force could have been expanded and, with

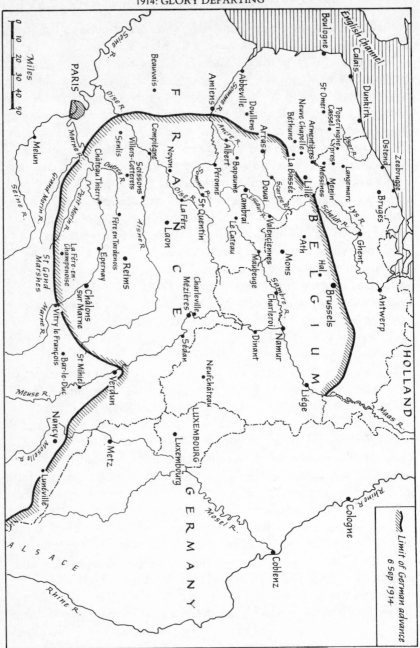

The Western Front, August–September 1914

little further training, have filled exactly the same role as the New Army (Kitchener's Army) for far less cost and administrative muddle. As it was, whole battalions of such fine officer material, like the London Scottish, to name only the First Territorial unit in the Ypres Salient, were hurled into the line as stopgaps, and a potential officer cadre was thus wiped out.

It would seem that the creation of an entirely new army, to be called Kitchener's Army, was an example of extreme egoism rather than the result of experience of French Territorials.

This criticism in no way reflects on those eager young men who later rushed to join Kitchener's Army. 'King and Country' needed them, as they were so pointedly told, and they responded nobly. Disillusion had had no time to set in. Later in the war a cartoon appeared to shame those unwilling to volunteer, under the caption 'What did you do in the Great War, Daddy?', a small boy asking the question of a rather sheepish-looking father. A cynic answered this question in a music-hall joke, 'He fought and fought and fought but he had to go in the end'. But it was the system that was wrong, not the men.

By efficient organisation, the Regular Army mobilisation which had begun in the afternoon of 4 August was followed by embarkation at Southampton only five days later. The BEF arrived in the concentration area around Maubeuge on the 20th. This feat is all the more remarkable in view of the large number of reservists that were needed to bring the battalions up to strength.

There was no mass-media to recall men to the colours. Telegrams, letters, and posters were the only means available. Defections were rare and the men were kitted out (not always a good fit) and moved to places of embarkation in an incredibly short space of time. The reception of the troops at the French ports, Le Havre being the main one, was ecstatic – 'It was roses, roses all the way'. Unaccustomed *vin ordinaire* played far less havoc than the endless demand for souvenirs, although a lack of cap badges would have done much to baffle lurking enemy agents.

The secrecy in which the BEF was carried to France aboard an average of thirteen ships a day, protected from afar by the Royal Navy rather than in close convoy; its safe arrival in France; and its whereabouts unknown to or only guessed at by the enemy, do little credit to the much-vaunted German spy – the bogey man of 1914. The absence of a German spy ring was another well-kept secret, since the whole network, largely through the stupidity of its members, was known to the security services from the outset.

GHQ embarked in the light cruiser HMS *Sentinel* on 14 August and, after a stop in Amiens, arrived in Paris on the 15th. In a round of official visits Sir John did not make a particularly good impression, but on the 16th at *Grand Quartier Général* (GQG) in Vitry-le-François, the two Commanders-in-Chief, exact contemporaries, met, and here there appears to have been a certain mutual admiration. Joffre succeeded in creating an atmosphere of cheerfulness and optimism which was felt throughout the whole of his headquarters. French was approved of by Commander and staff alike, and this approval was shared to an even greater extent by the populace, for wherever Sir John went he was most warmly received by the ordinary French civilians. Sir Archibald Murray, the Chief of Staff, was not so fortunate since wrestling with map references in the Lion d'Or Hotel at Paris, he was constantly interrupted by the incursions of the chambermaid. This would have had no particular significance had not Murray only been wearing his underpants.

The French have a strange streak of sentimentality, usually well concealed, and it may be that quite apart from the relief felt that the British were in the show, the name 'French' had something to do with the warmth of the Commander-in-Chief's reception. After all, no Frenchman is ever called 'English'.

Optimism was to be short-lived. As so often happens, there was trouble and disillusionment just round the corner, in this particular instance the result of both a clash of personalities and a disastrous strategical and tactical situation. These miseries can be summed up in one word – 'Lanrezac'. But before going into further explanations it is necessary to see how the overall situation had developed from the time of mobilisation of the French and German armies up to French's visit to Joffre on 16 August.

As can readily be seen, mobilisation and strategic plans cannot be changed at the last moment. Even without change they take much time to be put into operation. This timelag cannot be applied to British plans since the BEF was in no way comparable in size to the Continental armies, but had mobilised much later. Speed was of great importance to the Germans, but speed cannot be manufactured at will, and so a holding plan was devised in order to mask the concentration and advance of Colonel-General Alexander von Kluck's First Army (17 divisions or 260,000 men) on the extreme right wing. This holding force was composed of Lieutenant-General Georg von der Marwitz's II Cavalry Corps, which advanced towards the Meuse at Visé, and also a detachment from Colonel-General Karl von Bülow's Second Army (13 divisions or 260,000 men) which was to capture Liège, a Belgian fortress impregnable by certain standards due to its modern cupola-type fortifications.

It was at this place, fifty-four miles south-east of Brussels, that after several unexpected repulses by the gallant Belgian defenders a new name appears in the history of warfare, that of Major-General Erich Ludendorff. His dynamic leading of the assault enabled the Germans, aided by Austrian siege howitzers hurried across Europe for the purpose, to capture the town and outlying forts. Among the last to surrender was Liège's heroic defender, Lieutenant-General Gérard Leman.

The delay caused to the Germans by the defence of Liège has been both overestimated and underrated. Liège did not surrender until 16 August. The delay to von Kluck was at the most two days, but those two days were vital to the BEF, since the German First Army could well have been over the Mons-Condé canal, the eventual British defence line, and have caught them emerging from their concentration area. So far, but by so little, the British force had escaped the trap. Elsewhere, farther south, the French armies, after initial gains into Alsace and Lorraine, had been counter-attacked and driven back behind their fortresses. Joffre, even by 20 August, was still optimistic and was determined to advance 'whatever the circumstances'.

The Germans made their own mistakes largely due to the incompetence of von Moltke who, for dynastic reasons, had allowed the commanders of Fifth and Sixth Armies, the Crown Prince ('Little Willie') and Prince Rupert of Bavaria, to counter-attack the French and thus give them a breathing space behind their frontier defences, rather than to entice them farther forward and so carry out the original Schlieffen Plan. This breathing space allowed Joffre to realign certain divisions for an attempted strike at the German centre.

The 240,000-strong Fifth Army (14 divisions), under the previously mentioned General Charles Lanrezac, was held farther to the left in a counter-attack role. It was now in danger of envelopment by vastly superior forces moving to the north and west of the Meuse and in a salient position between Namur and Charleroi. Lanrezac was also expecting the BEF, less than half his army's strength, to come up on his left. He remained static in his HQ at Rethel.

The movements of the Germans after the fall of Liège must now be considered. The armies concerned in the 'Schlieffen wheel' from right to left, it will be remembered, were respectively First Army (von Kluck), Second Army (von Bülow) and Third Army (8 divisions or 120,000 men under General Max von Hausen). The First Army was of course the spearhead of the envelopment while the other two were to act as pivots for the wheel. Moltke, far behind the lines, was creating a fashion in distant headquarters. He decided on 17 August that in order to co-ordinate the advance he would put von Kluck under von Bülow's orders. As they were both difficult characters and mutually antipathetic this ill-advised move was bound to have repercussions. The immediate consequence was that von Kluck determined to ignore any orders that Bülow might give him. Then, on the 20th, he decided to detach a large force consisting of his two reserve corps for the investment of Antwerp, into which fortress the Belgian Army had now retired. This decision was to have decisive results in the future. Also on the 20th Brussels was occupied, the joy of the Kaiser greatly outweighing the strategic importance of that capital.

Again on 20 August, a move of far greater importance than the capture of Brussels was begun, namely the investment of Namur by von Bülow's Second Army. Namur, considered even stronger than Liège, surrendered on the 23rd, although most of the fifteen forts had fallen earlier. Once again Austrian siege guns had triumphed over so-called impregnable fortification – no costly infantry attacks were needed.

It is now necessary to go back in time to 16 August, the day of French's visit to GQG at Vitry-le-François. On this day all would seem to have been going well, but the following day was a veritable *dies irae*. Lanrezac, the commander of the Fifth Army, was the darling of French military thought, which was in effect Plan XVII, but like many 'paper' generals he was not to be such a success on the battlefield. He was warmly recommended to French by Joffre's headquarters and so, accompanied, needless to say, by Henry Wilson as interpreter and Grand Vizier, the BEF's C-in-C went on to Rethel full of high hopes. These hopes were to be swiftly dashed for Lanrezac, to do him justice, had been warning GQG of danger for some days without success.

French generals could at this time be roughly divided into the dapper and the sloppy. Lanrezac was a classic example of the latter kind, being fat, untidy and wearing a pince-nez which habitually became unstuck – a most unmilitary figure. In common, however, with all French generals, although sometimes well concealed for reasons of state, he disliked the British in general and their army in particular. *Perfide Albion* took an unconscionable time a-dying.

Albion's first act of perfidy was the late arrival of the BEF on the left of the French Fifth Army. In Paris one of the chief causes of complaint was that Sir John estimated its time of arrival as 24 August. This slowness of movement had produced consequent howls of protest, but now, due to some arithmetical providence, this date had become the 21st, still not soon enough, however, for General Hely d'Oissel, Lanrezac's chief of staff.

The next act in what might be called the French farce is well known since it has been so graphically described by the then Lieutenant Edward Spears in *Liaison 1914*. Spears, then a subaltern and so at a disadvantage with all the senior officers with whom he was to come in contact in the near future, was liaison officer at Fifth Army HQ. After the initial broadside Lanrezac appeared and seemed to be under considerable emotional distress. Liège had surrendered on the 16th and it was by now evident that not only was Plan XVII, if not in ruins, beginning to fall apart, but also that the German right hook was beginning to take very definite shape.

No record remains of what happened during the next half hour when the two commanders had a private *tête-a-tête*. As neither spoke each other's language (French could just manage a few '*plume de ma tante*' school-boy phrases), it defies imagination what passed between them in view of Lanrezac's anglophobia and French's automatic dislike of anyone who was neither a cavalryman nor a gentleman. Anyway, when at length they came into the staff room French crossed to a map on the wall and asked whether the Germans were going to cross the Meuse at Huy. This name is about as difficult for an Englishman to pronounce as is Haywards Heath for a Frenchman, but Wilson was equal to the occasion, as he was in translating into a more acceptable form Lanrezac's incredibly rude reply: 'Tell the Marshal that in my opinion the Germans have merely gone to the Meuse to fish'. French was not slow to realise the tone of voice in which this was said.

On his way to Paris Sir John had sent off 'Wully' Robertson, his Quartermaster-General, to set up HQ at Le Cateau and at the close of this disastrous day he himself went there and learnt the news not only of Grierson's death, which was bad enough, but also, two days later, that Kitchener had appointed Smith-Dorrien to command II Corps, which was far worse. As yet, however, there was, as Queen Victoria would have said, no depression in this house.

V

INTO THE BATTLE OF MONS
22-23 AUGUST

The 'Cockpit of Europe' has become so trite an expression for the exploitation of Belgium as a battlefield that there should be considerable hesitation before it is used even once more. Worn-out phrases unfortunately do have their uses, and this one is no exception to the rule. Armies have fought, marched and countermarched, or perhaps more accurately retreated, since the earliest times through the first half of this unfortunate country. Mons, Charleroi, Nivelles, Enghien, Hal must all have had a familiar ring to the various armies of Germany, France and England.

Marlborough's troops had a reputation for swearing, Wellington's probably did equally well, but no British army, until 1914 had the supreme advantage of having their chief opponent called Kluck. Ribald rhymes must have been too numerous to chronicle, but an unexceptional marching song 'Tipperary' seems to be the only survivor of the period and is of course ageless. Why 'Tipperary'? No definite explanation, as far as is known, has ever been given. Was it because of the predominantly Irish strain in the BEF, the existence of which has already been mentioned in connection with the Curragh Incident?

It has already been said that the BEF contained a high proportion of reservists but, contrary to what is sometimes thought, old sweats with Queen's and King's South African medals, however tender their feet might have been, only formed a part of the infantry. There were many young soldiers, no doubt some with falsified ages, whose feet must have suffered equally on the cobbled roads leading from the concentration area to they knew not where.

The cavalry and gunners were magnificently mounted, although remounts were scarce. The local inhabitants were amazed to see the men so often leading their horses. Such horsemastership was regrettably not a feature of French cavalry training and sore backs were a severe handicap to their movements, as will shortly be seen.

The fog of war would now seem to have descended in pea-soup strength on all the antagonists. The dangers of the situation were still quite unknown to French and British headquarters while von Moltke on the Rhine in faraway Coblenz, was completely out of touch with his two right-wing armies. The general situation was that the Germans had everywhere gained the initiative following the capture of Liège on 16 August. The remainder of von Bülow's Second Army was advancing to the River Sambre with its centre directed on Charleroi, Napoleon's concentration area in 1815. Much confused fighting took place on 22 August, but the outcome was favourable to the Germans who forced the crossing of the river.

According to Gabriel Hanotaux, the French military historian, Lanrezac wrote on the evening of the 22nd:

> My opinion is that the enemy has not shown any numerical superiority, though he has perhaps considerable forces in the vicinity. The Fifth Army is shaken as the result of the battle, but is still intact. If it has suffered heavy losses it has also inflicted heavy losses on the enemy. Having now been withdrawn into more open country, where the artillery of the Army which is still intact can act effectively, the Army should be able to bring the Germans to a stand. Our troops by defending every yard of the ground can give time to reorganise, and will shortly be in a position to counter-attack.

This dispatch seems to be a strange mixture of fact and fiction or, perhaps more correctly, wishful thinking. The German artillery, stronger in firepower and numbers (about 1000 guns, to 600) than the French, in spite of the famous 75s, would have even greater scope for destruction than its opponents. It is true, however, that Lanrezac still had considerable reserves as well as his I Corps, and the British were said to be supporting his left.

On the 23rd General von Plettenberg, the commander of the 41,000-strong German Guard Corps, was preparing to advance against the French, who had once more fallen back to a new position. A large French force was, during his preparations, reported on his left flank and consequently he had to postpone his attack to meet this threat. This force was the above-mentioned I Corps, which had handed over the defence of the Meuse at Dinant to a reserve division, and had now arrived on the Sambre battlefield.

Bad news then arrived for the French, first that Namur had fallen, and also that Dinant had been taken by a Saxon Corps of von Hausen's Third Army. General Louis Franchet d'Esperey's I Corps had therefore to make an about-turn to the Meuse to protect Lanrezac's right and rear. Had I Corps, almost 35,000 men and 132 guns, been able to attack the flank of the German Guards, the Battle of the Sambre might have had a very different result.

Only a few miles away lay Ligny, where on 16 June 1815 Napoleon had defeated Field-Marshal Prince Blücher, the Prussian commander. This defeat might have been total had not General Count Drouet d'Erlon's II Corps of 20,000 men marched and countermarched between Ligny and Quatre Bras as the result of order, counter-order and disorder. If Napoleon had had this reinforcement the Prussians might never have arrived on the field of Waterloo.

So much for Lanrezac's false hopes. By the evening of the 23rd his Fifth Army front had everywhere been driven in. The right flank was threatened by the capture of Namur and Dinant and General Sordet's Cavalry Corps of 13,500 men and 24 guns was ordered to move over to help to protect the British left. In view of the circumstances Lanrezac ordered a general retirement.

Strange events were taking place, however. Spears, the British liaison officer at Lanrezac's headquarters, had told Wilson of the true situation on the Sambre. Wilson had already tried to gloss over the fiasco at Fifth Army HQ in Rethel and now, on the 22nd, had persuaded French to have another meeting with Lanrezac. On the way, by a strange coincidence, they met Spears and were given the true picture. French returned to Le Cateau from whence he had come, possibly with some relief, and Spears went back to hear of worse perils for the BEF now that the Fifth Army was to retire and any idea of an offensive was off. The British were not even mentioned in the orders.

After a journey which lasted four hours due to appalling road conditions, Spears arrived at Le Cateau to find an order group busy with plans for a further advance into Belgium for the next day. The Subaltern made his report to the Field-Marshal. The outcome was that the plans for the morrow were off. No explanations were given, but the British Cavalry Division was ordered to move from the right to the left flank, that is the left flank of II Corps.

Later that night an officer arrived at Le Cateau from Lanrezac's HQ with the truly extraordinary request that the BEF should attack Bülow's right flank, extraordinary in view of the fact that on the same afternoon Lanrezac reported to GQG that the BEF had not even come upon his left. The truth was quite to the contrary, for the British were well forward of the French Fifth Army, already in retreat.

French, for his part, agreed to hold his present position for twenty-four hours but refused the request to attack. Knowing by now from Spears the true position, it is difficult to see how French could have envisaged the possibility of even a twenty-four-hour stand with his whole force out on a limb. He had two factors to weigh up that derived from his orders from HM Government. Firstly, not to endanger his command and second, to co-operate as far as possible with his ally. By this time the British C-in-C must have had a deep distrust of Lanrezac that would mitigate strongly against any form of action in conjunction with the French, and yet they could not be completely ignored, if he was to carry out the other part of his orders. He was in a cleft stick, and the trap was closing.

To restate the situation with regard to the BEF: even on the 21st, when it was marching towards an unknown destination, the Germans were across the Sambre at Charleroi. By the 23rd, when the Battle of Mons opened, they were some seven miles to the south of that place and thus well south of the British right. On the morning of the 24th, when the withdrawal from Mons had begun, the French Fifth Army was in complete retreat.

Mons, the capital of the Province of Hainault, had had a much troubled history. From a siege in 1425 onwards it had suffered military occupations, chiefly during the eighteenth century; Marlborough captured it in 1709. In 1815 it had sheltered Wellington's outposts and was a highly sensitive point from which to monitor Napoleon's movements. This monitoring had not been a conspicuous success due to the slowness of the Prussians in forwarding an intelligence report. 'He has humbugged me, by God!' said the Duke, a 'humbug' which had gained for Napoleon a lead of twenty-four hours.

The country in 1815 was very different from what it had become nearly a hundred years later. At the time of Waterloo it was rolling farmland, now it was an important part of the industrialised south of Belgium, having become a large mining district with all the obstacles to a defensive field of fire for the artillery such as slag heaps, rows of miners' cottages, and factories.

Neither the British nor the French had expected to fight in this unlovely country, so different from the training areas of Aldershot and Salisbury Plain. Both armies had hoped to be able to wheel northward and so be clear of the mining district. Once, however, the strategic initiative has been gained, the tactical battle has to be fought where and when the army with such an initiative chooses. The Germans were, more by chance than by good management, the choosers. The one thing that they did not know was the true whereabouts of the British Army, which, under the circumstances, says little for their intelligence service.

The BEF was now in position to fight on the following day what was to be called the Battle of Mons. Smith-Dorrien's II Corps of over 36,000 men and 152 guns held roughly the line of the Mons-Condé canal, while Haig's I Corps formed a refused right flank on the line Mons-Harmignies-Peissant.

On 21 August, the day before the start of the alarms and excursions, von Kluck's army was marching south-west from Brussels through the old areas occupied by British troops before Waterloo. He believed that the BEF might be advancing from the direction of Lille. Kluck's marches on the 21st were uneventful but, early on the 22nd, the first British shots of the land war were fired.

There now appears on the scene the almost legendary figure of Tom Bridges. The word 'almost' is perhaps unfair since the stories about him are substantially true, while other legends are true to this day only in the minds of a susceptible public. At this time Bridges, a major in the 4th Dragoon Guards, was commanding 'C' Squadron of that regiment on outpost duty at Casteau, about five miles north from Mons on the Soignies-Brussels road. Early in the morning of the 22nd a small party of German horseman, now known to be acting as divisional cavalry and not then part of von der Marwitz's II Cavalry Corps ranging far to the German right, was observed. They turned back before reaching 'C' Squadron. Bridges then ordered two troops (half a squadron or about eighty men) under Lieutenant Hornby to follow them up. In true *arme blanche* style they went off at full gallop down the road. They scattered what turned out to be a whole squadron (full strength was 169 men) of the 4th Cuirassiers, a strange coincidence not only in the regimental numbers but also in the similarity between dragoon guards and cuirassiers. The Germans, however, carried lances that proved completely useless in close combat. The upshot of the whole mêlée was that the enemy had considerable losses and rapidly decamped, while Hornby's two troops returned considerably elated having suffered no casualties.

To the north-east and east of Mons, between La Louvière and Binche, the 5th Cavalry Brigade acted as covering troops for I Corps, the regiments engaged being the Royal Scots Greys and the 16th Lancers. The Greys, in a dismounted action with two of their three squadrons, showed how valuable their training in the .303 rifle infantry had been, since the Germans withdrew with considerable loss.

A troop (about forty men) of 16th Lancers, in support of the Greys had, like the 4th Dragoon Guards, an opportunity to charge, but with the lance and in open country, and inflicted considerable casualties on scouting *Jäger* infantry. These brief encounters served to prove the superiority of the British Cavalry Division under Major-General Edmund Allenby in both mounted and dismounted action. They were of course the first indications the Germans had of the actual presence of British troops, but they were still unaware that the whole BEF was deploying both to the west and south-east of Mons. Even long after the Battle of Mons von Kluck believed that the BEF's bases were the Channel ports.

At dawn on Sunday, 23 August the German First and Second Armies had between them 150,000 men and 600 guns within striking distance of the British force of 70,000 men and 300 guns. Von Kluck was quite unaware of the landing of the major part of the British troops at Le Havre and their concentration area round Maubeuge. Due to this lack of information von der Marwitz's cavalry divisions were on a wide sweep beyond the River Escaut (Scheldt) with the extreme right corps of First Army ready to support them should they encounter the BEF from the direction of Lille. The march route of the First Army has already been mentioned, and the troops were strung out in their marching columns for miles along the roads so familiar to Wellington's men.

The simple precaution which von Kluck should have taken would

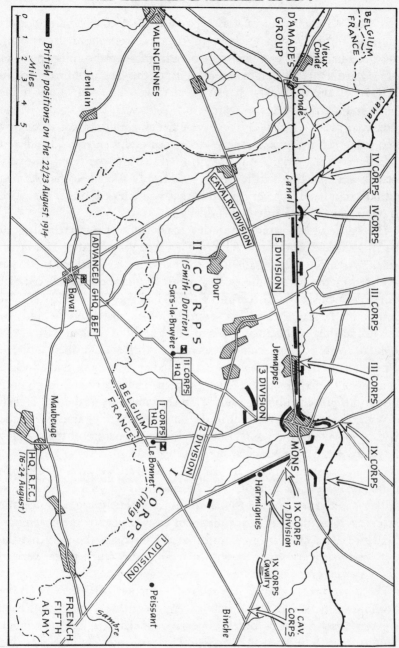

Mons, 23-24 August 1914

have been to deploy all of von der Marwitz's 15,600 cavalry and 24 guns, his three divisions of covering troops, well ahead of his main body, and not send the greater part on a fruitless errand thirty miles to his seaward flank. The chief consequence of this lack of information in the face of almost 11,000 British cavalry was that, with most of the German First Army force strung out as it was, there could be no concerted attack on the 23rd. All von Kluck could do was to deploy piecemeal such troops as happened to be nearest his enemy. The idea of a 'Contemptible Little Army' or of 'mercenaries', the term generally used to describe the British Army, was firmly rooted in the German military mind and it is very possible that von Kluck thought that such an opposition could easily be brushed aside.

The Battle of Mons opened with a bombardment by the artillery of the IX and III Corps of von Kluck's First Army. Soon after 11 a.m. an attack was made on the salient of the canal to the north of the town defended by the 4th Middlesex Regiment. (It must be remembered that some regiments in high recruiting areas had more than two regular battalions. In later days, of course, a 4th battalion would be Territorials, but at this time 3rd and 4th battalions formed part of the Regular Army. Other examples were the 4th Royal Fusiliers and 3rd Worcesters.) The Middlesex were attacked in front and flank by the equivalent of six battalions. The Germans came forward in column formations preceded by skirmishers, in the same way as did the French at Waterloo, and were seen off in the same way by the rapid fire of the British. In spite of the poor visibility due to the nature of the country the Royal Artillery gave what support it could.

The conclusions drawn by British observers at prewar German maneouvres who had speculated as to the result of such tactics against British rapid fire, were proved to be completely right, since the attacking formations at Mons made an easy target for the defenders' rapid fire. The story is often told that the Germans thought that the BEF was massively supplied with machine-guns when there were in fact only two in each battalion.

There had been a conference at Smith-Dorrien's HQ at 5.30 on the morning of the battle. What really went on at this conference is hard to determine. Accounts differ, especially, as may be well imagined, those of French and Smith-Dorrien. The probable outcome was that corps commanders were told to be ready either to retire, or to advance

50

which, in view of the known situation of German strength and French Fifth Army weakness, seems almost incredible. 'Almost' is perhaps the *mot juste,* since nothing is entirely incredible where Henry Wilson is concerned. He was obviously still trying to inject Sir John French with further false optimism. The latter therefore went off to inspect some newly-arrived troops as far away as Valenciennes, and took no part in directing the battle.

Even at 3 p.m., when the Field-Marshal returned to advanced GHQ at Bavai, he did not realise the extent of the German effort and still thought that the enemy were merely probing his outposts. During the afternoon French sent the following message to Lanrezac: 'I am prepared to fulfil the role assigned to me when the Fifth Army advances to the attack [*sic*]. In the meantime I hold advanced defensive positions ... I am now much in advance of the line held by the Fifth Army and feel my position to be as far forward as circumstances will allow, particularly in view of the fact that I am not properly prepared to take offensive action until tomorrow morning, as I have previously informed you.'

This report demonstrates Henry Wilson's influence. He had estimated that the BEF faced one corps and a cavalry division, which he must have known to be nonsense, and by persuading French that this was so was allowed to draft an order for an attack on the next day. Later that evening a message arrived from Joffre that the BEF was being threatened by three German corps. Sir John's optimism even extended to override this bad news, since he believed he could still advance on the following day. Due, however, to a further message from Smith-Dorrien, which gave the true situation as it affected II Corps, the plan of attack was altered to one of defence on the existing line.

The worst news of all arrived with Spears at midnight. Lanrezac, he had discovered, had issued orders for a withdrawal that would leave the right of the BEF even more in the air than it was. Since it seems that Spears had 'discovered' this information it was apparent that the British would have had no notice of this further retirement had it not been for Spears's curiosity. Lanrezac, it was said, was retiring in conformity with the French Third and Fourth Armies, which had met with near-disaster between Virton and Neufchateau farther to the south.

Poor French, he was the victim not only of his friends, in the shape of

Henry Wilson, but also of his enemies, who at this moment seemed to be far more the French than the Germans. This move by Lanrezac was to have disastrous effects on French and his subsequent moves since he became not only distrustful of this one individual, but also of his allies in general.

What had happened on the battlefield by then? Through sheer weight of numbers the Germans had been able to cross the canal to the east of Obourg, which is itself to the east of the salient, and so were able to make a pincer movement on Mons from the north and east. The British were then gradually pushed back to the south-east of the town. The main position of the 3rd Division, commanded by Major-General Hubert Hamilton, was south of Mons and in touch with I Corps at Harmignies, and it was to this location that the forward troops were withdrawn. The Germans had suffered such heavy losses that they could only consolidate their gains at dusk, and made no attempt to attack this main British position.

Hamilton's left brigade (the 9th) was attacked by the left division (6th) of the German III Corps and, farther west still, the right division (5th) of II Corps and also the forward elements of IV Corps. All were driven back, which enabled the line of the canal in this sector to be held until dusk when its defenders were withdrawn to a rear position. On the left of the whole line the cavalry and the 19th Infantry Brigade managed to hold their original positions against the few attacks made upon them.

Haig's I Corps was hardly engaged at all during this memorable day, due to the tardy progress of Bülow's VII Corps which, having reached Binche, was presumably concentrating in order to attack on the following day. To summarise the situation at the end of the 23rd, the two divisions of II Corps, overstretched on a twenty-one mile front, had been attacked during the whole of the day by three German corps, or over 120,00 men, whose only success had been to drive back the British outposts, sustaining enormous losses in doing so. A fourth German corps had been for a part of the afternoon within reach of the battlefield but had taken no part. If von Kluck had also pressed his attack later in the day of the 23rd the result of the battle might have been very different.

Since the enemy had been able to penetrate through the town of Mons, the British 3rd Division to the south-east of the town was in some difficulty. As its withdrawal to the main position took place earlier than 5th Division's, a gap developed in the centre into which German elements had infiltrated. Fortunately this gap was closed after dark, but had it been energetically exploited the situation might have become critical.

The firepower of the British with the rifle, combined with the weariness after long marches of the German troops, made for such confusion that the escape of the BEF was later made possible. Piecemeal attacks have ever ended in failure, and von Kluck's efforts in thus committing his vastly superior forces says little for his generalship.

What then was the true result of the Battle of Mons? It is too easy to say that it is a battle that should never have been fought; of course it should not have been fought. Kitchener was right. The BEF marched straight into a trap: 'The hands they were the hands of Kitchener, but the voice it was the voice of Henry Wilson'. In fact the great deception practised upon the military establishment by a smooth-talking Irishman, in his turn influenced by French delusions of the force of the attack over the firepower of the defence, neglected the lessons of as long before as the American Civil War.

The truest lesson learnt at Mons was that the 'invicibility' of the German Army was a myth. At Ligny they had been 'damnably mauled' but since then, after coming in at the death at Waterloo, they had had a succession of easy conquests in Denmark, Austria and France (1864-71). What they got at Mons was an unexpectedly bloody nose due to a lack of appreciation on their part of the firepower of the defence, properly trained in the use of small arms, over attacks in mass formation. The British could shoot, accurately and fast.

In crowing over the early British defeats in South Africa they had blinded themselves to the lessons to be learnt in a 'colonial war'. The British Army had suffered much at the hands of the Boers and presumably the legend that all Boers were crack shots had helped to improve the shooting in all arms of the service. As early as 1881, just after the disaster of Majuba Hill, a Boer leader had said to Sir Evelyn Wood about some of his compatriots, 'Great girls they can't shoot'; another had said that it was only as a result of constant practice that a high standard with the rifle could be kept up. Lord Roberts had appreciated this need for constant practice years before in his various commands in India and, later, as C-in-C in Ireland. After the Boer War, as

Commander-in-Chief of the Army, he had insisted on intensive training in what was somewhat whimsically called musketry throughout all arms of the service.

Mons was not a defeat. It can hardly be called a victory, although it is a battle honour borne on the colours of the regiments that took part. In truth, from the British side it is scarcely more that what used to be called an affair of outposts. This statement is only true of the 23rd, since more important fighting took place on the 24th, but that day should properly form part of the retreat because orders had been issued for a withdrawal on Bavai during the night before.

German generalship was seriously at fault. Von Moltke, far in the rear, had lost control. Von Kluck the Westphalian was furious at being put under the control of von Bülow the Prussian, his exact contemporary. Both were difficult characters and had no use for Moltke. First Army intelligence was non-existent and consequently von Kluck was unable to estimate the true strength and extent of the British positions, and then, knowing their weakness and in conjunction with Bülow, surround a comparatively small force that had both its flanks in the air. Much blame has been laid on the French Army for the Retreat from Mons. Lanrezac's cynical disregard of his ally was unforgivable but, whatever the immediate tactical situation on both the right and left of the BEF, retreat was inevitable due to the vast superiority in numbers and the enveloping movements of the two German armies.

French, the Commander-in-Chief, took no part in the battle. Smith-Dorrien handled his two divisions with determination and skill but I Corps was almost unaffected, except by artillery fire, and its casualties in *two* days, 23 and 24 August, were only 74. The losses suffered by II Corps, again over *two* days, were 4021 and, the cavalry, 257. Since on the 24th, the beginning of the withdrawal, the casualties were greater than on the 23rd, it can be easily seen that on the 23rd the 'butcher's bill' was comparatively light – probably about 1600 with two abandoned guns. It must also be borne in mind that, especially at the time of the withdrawal, orders did not reach certain pockets of resistance and the survivors, after expending all their ammunition, were forced to surrender and to suffer a long captivity.

These casualty figures, distressing as all such figures must be, are remarkably light and materially substantiate the 'affair of outposts'

54

contention. They also dispose of the legend that Mons was a battle in which the British suffered enormous losses.

Other legends are not so easily dispelled. To this day Mons is inevitably connected, in the minds of such members of the public that have ever heard of the battle, with angels – white shadowy figures who stood between the thin khaki line and the advancing hordes of the enemy, much to the latter's discomfiture. Bowmen, again intervening between the two armies, and friendly horsemen protecting the flanks of the retreat, also enter into the legendary history of this first encounter by a British army with a continental enemy in Europe for almost a hundred years. 'Angels and Ministers of grace defend us', said Hamlet; the angelic host is easily accounted for, but from whence came the bowmen and the horsemen? Crécy and Agincourt were a long way off. These points are academic, however, the facts of the matter are that these stories were widely believed at home, as was the story of great numbers of Russians being transported via England to the Western Front. They must have been Russian, people said, because they had snow on their boots. In this case a lucid explanation has been put forward that the 'Russians' were Highland soldiers, largely Gaelic speakers, who came from Ross-shire.

The other legends cannot simply be dismissed as inventions or propaganda, though they were of course used for propaganda purposes. The 'angels' rather obviously showed that the Almighty was on the side of right, which was British, rather than that of the German might. The other phenomena could not be so easily explained (the horsemen, friendly figures on the flanks, were authenticated by two quite senior officers). Be this as it may, the explanation of all these apparitions is more easily understood today, when so much is now known about battle fatigue and the effect of wounds on the 'heat-oppressed brain'.

In Italy during the Second World War a wounded soldier on an ambulance train going to the base hospital at Taranto said to his battalion CO, who was in similar circumstances: 'Did you know, Sir, that Colonel T ... was watching the battle, several of us saw him.' Colonel T was a very popular former CO of the same battalion who had been promoted. The facts were that Colonel T, although in Italy, was at the time at a base many miles from the battle. That the soldier was quite convinced that he had seen Colonel T is not in doubt, for he was well known as a steady character. Such are the effects of shock and fatigue, and they may perhaps help to explain these far more highly-coloured apparitions of 1914.

There is of course a more mundane explanation. In his book *The Great War and Modern Memory* (1975) Paul Fussell says that the whole 'angel' myth developed from a short story written by Arthur Machen in the *Evening News* of 29 September 1914. This story mentioned no angels at all but was a fictional account of shining bowmen from Agincourt coming to the aid of their hard-pressed countrymen. The word 'shining' was the cause of all the trouble. These fictional bowmen were soon transformed into angels, and what was written as fiction was soon credited as fact.

John Terraine says in the *Smoke and the Fire* (1980) that as early as 8 September Brigadier-General John Charteris, Haig's chief of intelligence, said in a letter that the story of the Angels of Mons was going strong through II Corps. 'Very soon', he says 'similar stories were appearing in the British Press, notably one by Arthur Machen entitled "The Bowmen" in the *Evening News* on 29 September. Machen substituted the bowmen of Agincourt for the Heavenly Host as allies against the "Prussian hordes" and claimed that his story was the unwitting origin of all the accounts of supernatural intervention in the Mons campaign.' Terraine goes on to say 'it was no such thing: General Charteris's letter preceded Machen's story by over three weeks', while the story already mentioned of the mystical horsemen appeared in the *Evening News* on 14 September, a fortnight earlier than Machen.

Paul Fussell also states categorically that it was not the Kaiser who had called the BEF 'a contemptible little army', writing that 'it is now known that the phrase emanated not from the German side but from the closets of British propagandists (*sic*) who needed something memorable and incisive to inspire the troops'. He goes on to say 'that the phrase was actually devised by Sir Frederick Maurice at the War Office and fathered upon the Kaiser'.

It is perhaps too academic to say that the word 'propaganda' did not come into popular use until much later, but there are other reasons for mistrusting the 'propaganda' theory for the phrase. In his book, Sir Frederick himself says 'when we landed in France ...' and goes on to describe his conversation with a French officer. According to the

Army List Maurice was a General Staff Officer at 3rd Division HQ, and at no time was at the War Office in 1914. *Brewer's Dictionary of Phrase and Fable*, however, states that the Kaiser's order is 'almost certainly apocryphal', said to have been given at Aachen on 19 August: 'It is my royal and imperial command that you ... exterminate first the treacherous English, and ... walk over General French's contemptible little army.'

'What is truth, said jesting Pilate' — it is to be noted that he did not wait for an answer.

VI

THE DELAYING BATTLE AT LE CATEAU 24-26 AUGUST

Withdrawal is not an unknown word in British military history, although BEF standing for 'back every fortnight' is perhaps more affectionate than derogatory. To win the last battle is the essential, but at what cost in the meantime? Since, however, withdrawal more usually means retreat, which is an unmentionable word in the military vocabulary, practice in such an art is seldom included in annual manoeuvres. To have made a withdrawal in daylight twice in three days in the face of a much superior enemy was no mean test, especially as the necessity for the second delaying action at, and withdrawal from, Le Cateau by Smith-Dorrien's II Corps is a matter of great controversy even today.

One reason for Kitchener's autocratic rule, often given, was that he had no adequate staff at the War Office to advise him, not that he would have accepted their advice anyway. All the best staff officers were presumed to be in France. Where they had disappeared to was at the time a matter of some mystery.

As has been said at the end of the last chapter, an order for withdrawal was issued during the night 23-24 August. This was actually issued to chiefs of staff at about 1 a.m. on the 24th, although the orders were as vague as was the staff work which produced them. Murray was already on the verge of breakdown, and such commands as appeared simply instructed the corps commanders to get on with a withdrawal under their own steam.

At the time of these orders the French Fifth Army was more than a day's march away on Haig's right. All the French troops, mainly Territorials on Smith-Dorrien's left and rear, were very scattered, so at the time when the retreat was ordered both flanks of the BEF were completely in the air. Haig, knowing the situation on his right, and because his corps had had virtually no fighting on the previous day,

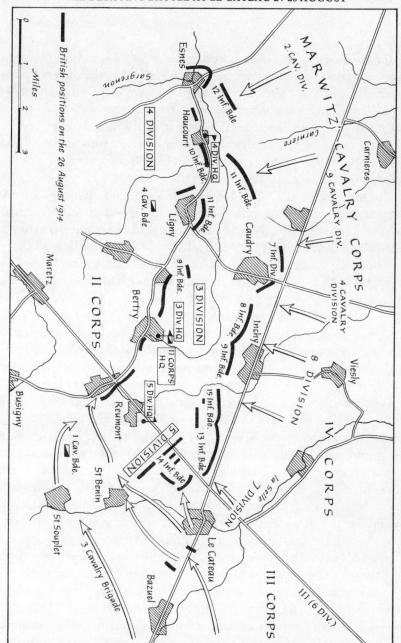

Le Cateau, 26 August 1914

was able to withdraw before the Germans were aware of what was going on.

On Smith-Dorrien's front, however, the situation was very different. To the south and south-west of Mons a heavy bombardment by the German IX and III Corps was followed by the now habitual attacks in mass. These attacks received the same treatment as they had on the previous day. The German IV Corps tried to encircle the Cavalry Division, the 19th Brigade and 5th Division between Pommeroeul and Condé, but much of the original force of the German attacks was lost since the retirement had already begun.

The alluring prospect of a fortress, even a second-class one, as very present help in trouble, was one to be resisted at all costs. Almost within sight, Maubeuge could well have had great attraction for a retreating army, but Sir John French had read enough military history to know the dangers of such a place of refuge. Retreat was therefore inevitable. Von Kluck had planned for a general attack on the morning of the 24th on the front and flanks of the British Army. The German advance was made with great caution in view of the losses they had already suffered, and the forts of Maubeuge also gave cause for concern since they could cover the right flank of Haig's I Corps. As a result the left of the First German Army was slow to follow up the retreating right flank of the BEF and consequently I Corps and the 5th Cavalry Brigade, which had covered the retirement, had by nightfall reached a line between Maubeuge and Bavai and were scarcely engaged. Likewise, the right of II Corps, 3rd Division, after its successful action south-west of Mons, was able to retire unmolested.

Unfortunately, on the left flank there was a different story to tell. The 5th Division, the Cavalry Division and 19th Infantry Brigade were in action against three divisions of III and IV German Corps, while von der Marwitz's cavalry, back under von Kluck's orders, was making a flanking movement to cut off the BEF from its still-supposed bases of Calais and Boulogne. During the morning of the 24th between the Condé canal and the southern limits of the mining villages south-west of Mons, a running fight ensued in which the masses of the enemy tried to work round the British left flank. It was in this action that part of 5th Division suffered its heaviest casualties and pockets of resistance, often not having received orders to retire, were inevitably made prisoners.

Von Kluck's IV Corps, in their efforts to outflank the British left, suffered such enormous losses in their ponderous attacks that even their superiority in numbers failed against the firepower of the British infantry and their gunners, often firing over open sights. The remainder of 5th Division also stopped in its tracks its German opposite number, the 5th Division of III Corps, which was in consequence quite unable to follow up the retreat.

Perhaps the most epic combats of this long hot day occurred round the village of Audregnies when the 5th Division flank guard and 2nd Brigade of the Cavalry Division took the full force of the turning movement by the German IV Corps mentioned above. Trying to advance southward across the Mons-Valenciennes road a column of German infantry, about the strength of a regiment (the equivalent of three battalions or 3300 men), was deploying for an attack when 'L' Battery RHA's six 13-pounders came into action from behind a hedge, almost unsupported, and under fire from four heavy German batteries kept the enemy at bay for about three hours. They only withdrew when their ammunition was exhausted. They had not lost a gun.

It has already been said that pockets of resistance held out to the very last round, often as a result of orders not having been received to withdraw. Three-quarters of the Cheshire Regiment, who did at least have one machine-gun, held up a German attack similar to the one mentioned above until dusk. When at last they were overpowered after three hours' fighting there were only some forty unwounded men who, in the words of one of them, 'were weary of slaughter'.

The sorely tried left flank, shepherded by Allenby's cavalry, who once more both in their mounted and dismounted action outfought their opponents, crossed back into France by the evening in line with the remainder of the BEF, the front extending westwards on the line La Longueville – Bavai – Jenlain, that is, along the main road from Maubeuge to Valenciennes.

On the right flank of the British Army, the French Fifth Army was *twelve miles away to the south-east*. On the left flank sundry French Territorial units were scattered over the countryside. Sordet's cavalry were still nursing sore backs or unable to cross the congested lateral roads; not surprising when a British infantry division with all its transport occupied fifteen miles of road. Both British flanks were thus still in the air. And so the evening and the morning were the first day.'

The next enemy to be overcome on the second day of the retreat was the Forest of Mormal. This vast obstacle was said to be impassable. True or not, since there was not time in which to make a sufficient reconnaissance, impassable it was considered to be. It was therefore decided to use such roads as existed to the east and west of the forest; I Corps being assigned to the east in the direction of Landrecies, and II Corps in the direction of Le Cateau by the roads to the west.

By this time the Germans must have been aware not only of the strength of the BEF, but also of the continued retreat of the French Fifth Army. By rights von Kluck should have had the British at his mercy, but human nature is only capable of just so much. His First Army had covered great distances on foot and had suffered far heavier casualties than they had ever believed possible at the hands of the 'contemptible little army'. Respect had replaced contempt and the one thing that they could and would not do was hurry. The leading units had therefore halted some six miles from the British outposts, as also had von der Marwitz's cavalry on the German right.

Early on the 25th the retreat from Mons was continued without great interference from the enemy. South-east of Valenciennes a long-range fight between the Cavalry Division and German divisional cavalry took place, but the enemy were unable to make any progress against the flank of II Corps marching towards positions on the Le Cateau-Cambrai road.

Later in the day the rearguard of 3rd Division was attacked by von der Marwitz's cavalry and the right of the German IV Corps. This small force in a defensive position near Solesmes had no cavalry protection, since Allenby's division was moving to try to fill the gap between the two corps caused by the Forest of Mormal. In Solesmes the situation was chaotic due to a mixup of transport, refugees, and lost French Territorials. A great chance was missed by the Germans, but they too were tired and were in no mood to fight against a determined defence. The two battalions of Wiltshires and South Lancashires, with the support of a battery of artillery, held their position until dark by which times the roads were cleared. The small rearguard, which had started at 3 a.m. that morning, reached their billets at midnight. The Germans made no further effort.

To the east of the forest German forward troops had, unlike the British, found passable roads through the woods and had attacked

62

Haig's I Corps at Maroilles and Landrecies. Such then in outline was the tactical situation. But what was going on behind the scenes?

Field-Marshal French, if he had not already started to 'flap', was seriously considering a long withdrawal, and this line of thought was summed up in a message to Lanrezac as early as the 24th, in which the BEF C-in-C stated that, if his left flank should be seriously threatened, he would retire on his line of communications, which in effect would do to Lanrezac what Lanrezac had done to him. Joffre, the unflappable, only asked French to delay the enemy as best he could. Sir John in reply said that he would do just that, more out of consideration for Joffre in particular rather than from any desire to help his allies in general. A position round Le Cateau was discussed with Murray and Wilson. Wilson, for once pessimistic, was actually suggesting that the Germans, moving round the left flank, were trying to cut the British communications. French disagreed, but wished to retire in conformity with the French Fifth Army and *'if necessary to get behind the Oise to reorganise and refit'*. Such was the Field-Marshal's thinking even on 25 August.

As has already been seen, the retreat during this day, especially that of I Corps, had gone without serious incident. II Corps, except for the rearguard of 3rd Division, had not been seriously engaged either. There would hardly seem to have been any undue cause for alarm. GHQ moved from Le Cateau to St. Quentin later on the 25th, and orders were issued to continue the retreat on the 26th.

In the early hours of the morning the news that Haig was being heavily attacked at Landrecies reached GHQ. It must be remembered that neither at Mons nor during these two subsequent days of retreat had I Corps been seriously engaged. What had happened was that the 4th Guards Brigade was surprised in its billets, the German leading troops entering the town dressed in French uniforms and answering any challenges in French. After some severe street fighting in which the Coldstreamers distinguished themselves the Germans were driven off, but the usually calm Haig had been badly shaken and had sent an alarmist report to GHQ, which had asked II Corps to come to the rescue. Smith-Dorrien refused, which was just as well in view of what was about to happen on the following day. It did not endear him either to French or Haig. After all, Smith-Dorrien's corps had borne the brunt of the fighting, with over 4400 casualties, and the situation at

Landrecies proved to be far less alarming than Haig had made out.

And so 'the evening and the morning were the second day'. In the early morning of the 26th Haig's I Corps continued its retreat, orders having been issued to both corps to continue their retirement at daybreak. Haig's command marched off in the direction of Guise, in touch at last with the French, Fifth Army; Smith-Dorrien's Corps did not retire.

After midnight on the 25th-26th Smith-Dorrien found that many of his troops had only just come in, and were in certain sectors still in close contact with the enemy. His appreciation of the situation was based on three main factors.

First, soon after midnight Major-General Allenby informed him that as his cavalry division was much scattered and men and horses tired, he could not continue to cover the retreat. The Germans, he stated, were in close contact with the British outposts and, if the troops were to be withdrawn, it would be necessary to do so under cover of darkness, which was by then an impossibility. Second, Hubert Hamilton stated that his 3rd Division could not continue its march before 9 a.m.

A third consideration was of even greater importance. The 4th Division, commanded by Major-General T.D'O. Snow, had been released by Kitchener, for reasons best known to himself, from home defence duties and had just arrived in France on 23 August. This division had detrained at Le Cateau on the 25th and Snow, although under no necessity to do so, had placed himself under Smith-Dorrien's command. With these three factors in mind the Corps Commander issued orders to stand and fight on the ridge which runs south of the Le Cateau-Cambrai road. By so doing he hoped that German pressure could be eased and that the BEF could be extricated from its critical situation.

The Germans on entering Le Cateau found the town full of British troops. Further probing established the fact that the line Caudry-Wambaix was also held and supported by artillery. In the confused fighting that followed the Germans gained enough information to realise that the British were in force and were no longer retiring.

The Germans, with the exception of von der Marwitz's cavalry, having experienced the effects of the British rifle fire, relied largely on their artillery to soften up the infantry positions and also headquarters and command posts sited in villages. These villages, since there had been no time to turn them into proper defensive positions, proved to be excellent aiming points for enemy artillery and generally had to be abandoned. It was also unfortunate that the troops (except for the newly arrived but still incomplete 4th Division) which had suffered the most during the retreat had to bear the brunt of the enemy attacks. In principle, however, by the early afternoon the whole line, which had already suffered attacks by vastly superior numbers for seven or eight hours, was still intact, which in itself was a *prima facie* case for the justification of the stand.

Von Kluck at the outset of the battle was in a position to know that Haig's I Corps was still falling back and that in consequence there was a wide gap between the two British corps. The British left was still some distance from the town of Cambrai, which was held by a French Territorial force. The German commander was therefore well placed, with a superiority of more than two to one (140,000 men to 55,000, plus token French help), to envelop both flanks. Smith-Dorrien could expect no help from I Corps, for obvious reasons, in spite of an earlier plan that both corps should make a stand at Le Cateau. The French were static in Cambrai. He had therefore by afternoon no alternative but to order a retirement, since in his opinion his men had more than accomplished their task of delaying the enemy's advance.

The decision for a second withdrawal in the face of a vastly superior force and in daylight was as difficult to make as was the decision to stand and fight. Complete success was almost secured except in the case of the 5th Division, which had already been severely tried, and in endeavouring to hold an attack by fresh enemy troops was driven back, thus anticipating orders for withdrawal. Other German units were slow to appreciate this success and consequently the withdrawal, covered by the artillery, was made with only small losses thanks to further fortuitous circumstances. As was so often the case since the 23rd, orders to retire had not reached various groups. These groups, which varied in size, held out to the last and thus largely aided the withdrawal since the enemy, being held up by their fire, were unable to pursue and were thus completely deceived until the main bodies were well away.

Once again von Kluck missed a great chance. Always obsessed with the idea that only a turning movement could bring a decisive victory, he marched off to the south-west while II Corps continued its retreat to the south. Once more von Kluck had all the forces and the tactical advantage necessary for the complete eclipse of the enemy, but he relied on his artillery and used only two of his nine available infantry divisions. Once more the Colonel-General had failed to exploit a great opportunity. He was not a great commander.

The most significant failure was that of the German cavalry. An attack by a fresh division, which had had ample time to rest, water and feed both men and horses, might have been decisive. After the early morning no cavalry appeared at all and later in the day they moved off in the direction of Cambrai, away from the British line of retreat. It was still possible that von Kluck thought that the BEF's bases were Calais and Boulogne. This day, 26 August, was the anniversary of the Battle of Crécy (1346), and as that battle marked the continental emergence of the longbow as a battlewinner, as well as the first recorded appearance of field guns, so Le Cateau was another landmark in the history of the Royal Artillery, since it marks the beginning of any study of the use of modern field artillery. II Corps' 226 guns outfought 340 heavier German pieces. Perhaps for this reason this battle has been called 'an encounter between nineteenth-century minds and twentieth-century weapons'. It was also the first battle of any magnitude that the British had fought on the continent since Waterloo, and indeed the largest all-British Army battle ever yet fought abroad.

The question which must be asked, however, is whether it should have been fought at all? Was Sir Horace Smith-Dorrien justified in the action which he took? As has already been seen, French issued orders to both corps to continue the retirement on the 26th. Haig obeyed, Smith-Dorrien did not. How far was the Commander of II Corps justified in so doing? He had issued his orders to continue the retreat before the representations were made to him by Allenby and Hamilton. Very early in the morning of the 26th, therefore, Smith-Dorrien told French of the situation and the Commander-in-Chief replied 'that if you can hold your ground the situation is likely to improve ...'. The only qualification was that 'Although you are given a free hand as to the method this telegram is not intended to convey the impression that I am not anxious for you to carry out the retirement and you must make every endeavour to do so.' Under the circumstances Smith-Dorrien felt that his action was justified.

Wilson had woken French at about 5 a.m. as soon as Smith-Dorrien's message had arrived. It would appear that at first French agreed, but later he told Wilson to urge Smith-Dorrien to break off the action as soon as he could. Wilson, however, was so impressed with Smith-Dorrien's confidence that he wished him good luck, saying 'yours is the first cheerful voice I have heard for three days.' French later never admitted having sent the telegram, always maintaining that he had urged Smith-Dorrien to retire as soon as he could. In the official dispatch French praised Smith-Dorrien to the skies, but excused it later by saying that the full facts were not then known (early September).

The whole controversy was of course a conflict of personalities, one that was to rage into 1915 and until French died. An impartial Commander-in-Chief would have judged the action by its results and not falsified the casualty figures to back up his contention that its commander had imperilled II Corps. French stated that the casualties were 14,000 men and 80 guns; the actual figures were 7,812 men and 38 guns. Only about forty per cent (3124) were due to enemy shellfire. Large numbers of stragglers were later able to rejoin their units but of course many prisoners were taken from those units, of varying sizes, that had not received orders to withdraw.

Perhaps the justification for the stand of II Corps at Le Cateau is that thereafter 'the retreat from Mons was not again seriously molested'. And so 'the evening and the morning were the third day'.

ONE BATTALION'S LE CATEAU: 24-26 AUGUST

The 2nd Battalion The Essex Regiment, forming part of 12th Brigade, 4th Division, which had been held back in England as part of Kitchener's defence against invasion, arrived in Le Havre at 10 p.m. on 23 August and landed at 5 a.m. on the 24th. At 10 a.m. the battalion's 1000 men were entrained and by 8 p.m. that same day they were at Bertry station south-west of Le Cateau. As has already been seen the situation was becoming critical, and 4th Division was pushed forward to protect the left flank of the BEF. At 5.30 a.m. on the morning of the 25th, close to the village of Viesly, a mile north of the Cambrai-Le Cateau road, they came in contact with the enemy. Heavy gun and rifle fire was heard to the west and shells were seen bursting on a ridge to the west of the village. There was no news but considerable anxiety was not allayed by the war-worn appearance of the 19th Brigade, originally on the left of the line, which passed through during the day.

The whole line was in movement and the 2nd Essex had a strenuous and exhausting time on the night of the 25th. Its parent division had been ordered to take up a position on the left of II Corps between Fontaine-au-Pire and Wambaix, with the reserve at Haucourt. At 8.30 p.m. 'C' and 'D' Companies under the CO were detailed as escort to the divisional ammunition column (whose 709 transport horses needed almost one-and-a half miles of road) with orders to halt at Bethencourt, waiting till the whole of 4th Division had passed through, and then to form the rearguard of 12th Brigade. 'A' and 'B' Companies with the regimental transport were advance-guard to the Brigade and arrived at Longsart near Esnes (both west of Haucourt) at 3.54 a.m. on 26 August, followed by the 2nd Lancashire Fusiliers.

The rearguard marched towards Haucourt with French cavalry actively reconnoitring to the north. Esnes was reached at 4.30 a.m. and orders were received to remain in reserve. Coffee was shared with a troop of French cavalry. It was now that Smith-Dorrien decided to make a stand and in this decision he was supported by Major-General d'Oyly Snow. who put 4th division under command. Soon after 6 a.m. sounds of heavy firing came from the right where the 5th Division was engaged in a fight for its very existence.

The British line was on the left of the River Selle between Le Cateau and Cambrai. The 4th Division did not arrive in its allotted position to the west of II Corps from Fontaine-au-Pire to Wambaix (a front of three miles) until after daylight on the 26th. They were of course tired, having come straight from England, detrained at Le Cateau on the 24th, marched eight or nine miles to Solesmes, been in action there all day and marched back over ten miles in the dark to their position, which was reached after dawn on the 26th.

On the right, south of Fontaine-au-Pire, was 11th Brigade, with 12th on the left about Longsart Ridge, which was covered with beetfields and cornstooks. The 10th Brigade was in reserve at Haucourt. The 11th Brigade was engaged in heavy fighting for some hours but the 2nd Essex in 12th Brigade held the extreme left of the line of the British Army. 'A' and 'B' Companies, 500 strong, were entrenched on the left on Longsart Ridge, 'B' in the front line and 'A' in support. The 2nd Lancashire Fusiliers were on their right and on the right of the Fusiliers were the 1st King's Own Royal Lancaster Regiment, who had reached Haucourt at 4 a.m., and after a short rest on the road had at about 5.45 a.m. moved up to extend the line. Two companies of the 2nd Royal Inniskilling Fusiliers were in support of the Lancashire Fusiliers, the other two companies being in brigade reserve with the remainder of the Essex, in and about Esnes.

The most prominent feature of the landscape, as viewed from Battalion HQ south of the Esnes-Haucourt road, was the clear outline of the ridge which bends inwards towards Esnes. A small ravine-like hollow marked the side of the ridge and to the right was the farm of Longsart set among trees. Still father to the right on the Esnes-Haucourt road was a sugar factory, also surrounded by trees. There was a clear view to the right as far as Haucourt and in the distance to the east Ligny could be seen, while to the left the rolling country beyond Esnes down to the River Escaut was also visible. There was open ground in front of the units of 12th Brigade for some distance.

Shortly after 6 a.m. two French troopers riding forward were seen suddenly to turn and gallop at top speed to the south-west. The enemy were advancing in force, being the 2nd Cavalry Division (about 5000 men) with two *Jäger* battalions (about 1300 light infantry). At that moment overwhelming machine-gun fire broke upon the front of 12th Brigade, striking the King's Own and the right of the Lancashire Fusiliers. The latter had entrenched but the King's Own, unwisely believing French cavalry protected their front, were caught in the act of sleeping before digging in and suffered twenty-eight per cent casualties, including a dead CO. The men rallied and replied with accurate rifle fire, but the six cavalry machine-guns firing from 800 yards were supplemented by twelve German 77mm field-guns which came into action and swept the King's Own. Two companies of the Royal Warwicks tried to reinforce them but were fired on as the King's Own had been, and the survivors of the two regiments took post in a lane on a reverse slope north of Haucourt. The Lancashire Fusiliers held firm but suffered severely as the enemy crept round and enfiladed them from the left, which also caused casualties to the two Essex companies and two companies of the Inniskilling Fusiliers which had reinforced the flanks of the Lancashire Fusiliers.

To the west of Esnes the remaining two companies of the Inniskilling Fusiliers were giving valuable help in hindering the effort to outflank. About 8.45 a.m. it was decide to vacate the ridge. The King's Own were the first to move, covered by a counter-attack made by two companies of the 1st Royal Warwickshire Regiment. The Lancashire Fusiliers were the next to withdraw under cover from fire by 'A' and 'B' Companies of the Essex. A battalion of German reserve infantry also appeared along the Essex front in close column but were promptly stopped by rifle fire. All of 12th Brigade was, however, able to withdraw without further molestation.

The noise of the firing at 6 a.m. aroused instant activity in Esnes and 'C' and 'D' Companies stood to. A French trooper dashed into the village and gave the CO a message, saying that 12th Brigade was being driven back. He at once ordered an advance to the sugar factory to cover the retirements of the other units. In this position the remains of 'A' Company gradually formed up on the right of 'D' Company and 'B' on the left. The preparations to resist attack were calmly and methodically made, even down to the issue of range charts to platoons (four of fifty-three men each made up a company). A company of the Inniskillings in Esnes protected the left flank of the Essex. When the Germans attempted to move forward again 'C' and 'D' Companies immediately opened fire at the extreme range of 1300 yards and checked their advance, which died away by 11 a.m. The CO of the Battalion, Colonel Anley, who was watching from higher ground later, said that the fire even at this long range was most effective on the enemy supports (unseen by those in the low ground) that were moving forward in close formation.

The new line taken up by 12th Brigade ran from Ligny through Haucourt to Esnes. It was also held by 10th Brigade, originally divisional reserve, so there was considerable intermingling of units. The Essex were about 500 yards in rear of their previous position, there being a better field of fire. About 1 p.m. an advance was made to Longsart Farm, the enemy apparently having evacuated the hill. Many killed and wounded were found there, but as the Germans opened a heavy fire the troops were ordered to retire again to the Haucourt-Esnes road.

The Essex found among the German dead many *Jäger* with the same Gibraltar badge on their caps which they themselves bore. It was the 10th Hanoverian Battalion, which had been comrades of the old 56th Foot in the defence of that fortress during the

Great Siege of 1779-83. The shelling was maintained, but did little damage this time as the missiles passed over the heads of the troops lying in the valley. About 3 p.m. a number of German guns appeared on the ridge NE of the farm and soon afterwards there was a heavy bombardment on Haucourt village. The German 2nd Cavalry Division was being reinforced by the IV Reserve Corps. An Essex company commander wrote:

The Brigade was lying down in a long line on the forward slopes of the low hills south of the road. In front of us and dominating our position lay the ridge from which we had been driven in the morning, except for a company of Inniskillings who were still gallantly maintaining their position on the extreme left. Through my glasses I saw the German guns gallop over the skyline, unlimber and open fire. The shrapnel caught the right of the Brigade and began sweeping along the line towards my position on the left flank. Unsupported to any extent by artillery fire and with the enemy's guns beyond effective rifle fire the centre and right began to move. I told my company we should have to go back, but we should do so at a walk. The shrapnel caught us as we went off, certainly as a rule bursting too high, but putting a severe strain on men who had never been under fire before. Not a man attempted to run. We passed two of our guns, the only ones I saw that day, the subaltern in command explaining he had just time to give them two more rounds.

About 5 p.m. came the final withdrawal of the 2nd Essex. The march of two and a half miles across open country was a most difficult task but when the men reached Selvigny village they formed up with absolute steadiness. Selvigny was to be held at all costs, but hardly had 'C' and 'D' Companies begun to entrench on the left flank when, at 6.20 p.m. the order came to retire again,so these two companies had to make their way almost eight miles across country in the rain to Vendhuille. There the remainder of the Battalion was sleeping, the advanced guard having arrived at 10.30 p.m.

The casualties of 12th Brigade were over a thousand, or more than a quarter of its strength, and of this total 141 were from the Essex. Theirs had been a gruelling baptism of fire.

VII

DECEPTIONS OF A RETREAT
26-29 AUGUST

The night and day following Le Cateau, II Corps, battered but unbowed, marched miles. Haig's I Corps, on the right, continued on their way if not rejoicing, at least relieved that it was Landrecies and not Le Cateau that they had had to suffer.

The French troops in Cambrai were from the 84th Territorial Division, a very new formation, and had been forced to retreat to Bapaume during the Le Cateau fighting. They were then joined by two reserve divisions, detached from the garrison of Paris, under General Albert d'Amade, and a further retirement was made to Peronne, a full twenty-two miles south-west of Cambrai. At long last the French cavalry under General Sordet had managed to cross the roads blocked by both the French and British retreats and on the 26th his cavalry corps was south of Cambrai, where its twenty-four guns helped to cover the British retreat on that day. On the 27th Sordet was able to delay the advance of von der Marwitz but on the 28th he and the two reserve divisions were attacked near Peronne, and compelled to fall back on Amiens.

The Commander of II Corps colourfully likened the immediate retirement of his troops from the Le Cateau battle to a crowd coming away from a race meeting. It was now that the whereabouts of the missing staff officers became known; they were with the lower formations. Their efforts to channel a fairly disorganised crowd not only in the right directions, but also to their particular units, was beyond praise. Sir William Robertson, the BEF Quartermaster-General, who had always anticipated a retreat, had done much to lessen the rigours of the long march by dumping supplies at the side of the roads.

When proper cohesion had been obtained, Smith-Dorrien marched straight for the Somme through St Quentin and by roads west of that town. By early on the 28th he had crossed the river at Ham, having

72

covered thirty-five miles from his battlefield. The cavalry covered the retreat with great skill, but nevertheless, for the infantry, which had fought a hard battle and had to march day and night, it was an exhausting effort, although spared from any serious rearguard action.

On the 27th the I Corps, now followed by formations of von Bülow's Second Army, suffered the loss of the greater part of the 2nd Battalion of the Royal Munster Fusiliers in a twelve-hour rearguard action fought at Etreux on the Oise by 1st Division. The stand made by this battalion aided by 'A' Squadron of the 15th Hussars, enabled the rest of the corps to continue on its way without difficulty. On the 28th the German cavalry did at last make efforts to follow up the retreat in some strength, but once again the British showed their superiority both mounted and dismounted, and thus enabled the infantry to complete their marches without molestation.

On the evening of the 28th the I Corps stood between the Gobain Forest and the River Oise, with II Corps north of the Oise at about Noyon. And so 'the evening and the morning were the fourth and fifth days'.

This rather bald account of the continuation of the retreat has in no way reflected the agitation at GHQ. French was breathing out threatenings and slaughter against Smith-Dorrien for ruining II Corps, as the C-in-C believed. Haig, suffering from the reverse at Landrecies, also considered that the decision to fight at Le Cateau was wrong; this seems to have been the general opinion at GHQ. History has, however, thought otherwise. The bad feeling between French and Smith-Dorrien, which continued even after the war, resulted in the latter's dismissal in April 1915; the sentence pronounced in those immortal words of 'Wully' Robertson, "'Orace you're for 'ome.'

On the 26th French met Joffre and Lanrezac at St Quentin. Bad feeling abounded. Joffre produced a new plan which he unfolded, as he thought, for a second time, since he believed that French was in possession of all the facts. This plan consisted in the formation of a new French Sixth Army at Amiens. The order, called *Instruction Générale No. 2*, had been received at GHQ, but had not been shown to French as Wilson had neglected to do so and Murray had collapsed. There was little real faith at GHQ in the new plan since French was determined to continue the BEF retreat, even if his left, considered to be the dangerous flank, was reinforced.

On the afternoon of the 26th GHQ was at Noyon, where a spirit of gloom still prevailed. The BEF, according to Huguet, the French liaison officer, was in disorderly retreat and had lost all contact with the Fifth French Army; in fact the situation, as has already been seen, was quite the contrary.

During the 28th GHQ moved back as far as Compiègne. Sir John went out to see for himself the condition of the men after five days of retreat. To use his own words, was 'agreeably surprised' at how well they were shaping, but in no way was he deterred from continuing the retirement and he refused to co-operate with Lanrezac in a counter-attack, convinced as he was of Lanrezac's duplicity and also of the BEF's need for rest and re-equipment.

There were two main circumstances which, after the Battle of Le Cateau, contributed to the comparatively feeble pursuit of the British Army. Both these limitations had existed from the original encounter at Mons. First and foremost was von Kluck's stubborn refusal to appreciate the true situation of his opponents and the direction of their retirement, and second was von Moltke's lack of control from his far-distant headquarters. The German Supreme Command, like British GHQ, thought that the British Army, and especially II Corps, were in disorderly retreat. The first report, dated 27 August, said: 'The English Army to which three French territorial divisions were attached has been completely defeated to the north of St Quentin; it is in full retreat. Several thousand prisoners have been taken ...'

Then again, on 29 August:

The latest defeat of the English near St. Quentin has been brought about by the fact that our masses of cavalry pursuing the English in their retreat towards St. Quentin forced them to stand and thereby enabled our army corps to intervene a second time in a decisive manner. The defeat of the English is now complete. They are completely cut off from their communications and can no longer escape by the ports at which they disembarked.

Lastly, on 31 August: 'The English Army is retiring on Paris in the most complete disorder and its losses are estimated at 20,000 men.'

It must be remembered that these were official reports from von Kluck to von Moltke. He obviously believed that he had gained a devastating victory, which only serves to show how deceptive the discarded impedimenta of a retreating army can be. Neglected dumps of food and material, together with wrecked vehicles and abandoned guns (in fact 42 out of an establishment of 404) and in addition, it must be said, a comparatively large number of prisoners (approximately 4000), would, taken all together, give an impression of a disorderly retreat unless the full facts were known.

When news filtered to German officers and men, even wilder stories appeared. Two diary entries will suffice: 'We hear [24 August] that the British cavalry has been annihilated and that six English divisions have been exterminated as they were detraining'. And, from a true German sentimentalist four days later:

This evening we had news of victories gained by von Bülow's Second Army; our souls were filled with joy when the regimental bands played the Hymn of Praise by the light of the moon and of the bivouac fires, and the tune was taken up by thousands of voices. There was general rejoicing and jubilation and when next morning [29 August] we continued it was in the hope that we should celebrate the anniversary of Sedan [1 September 1870] before Paris.

What would the British have sung under like circumstances?

The true situation was as follows, and was seemingly as obscure to GHQ as to the Kaiser. First I Corps had hardly been engaged. The long marches were both tiring and frustrating since the troops could not really understand the reason for the continual retirement not, as they thought, having been defeated in battle. The cavalry had performed with considerable success in all the clashes they had had with the enemy, but men and horses were tired. With II Corps the situation was different. Both 3rd and 5th Divisions had had two battles followed by two difficult withdrawals in the face of very superior enemy forces. They had suffered heavy casualties, it is true, but not to a crippling extent considering the circumstances. They had every reason to be tired as their withdrawals from action were of necessity followed by long and trying marches.

There was now III Corps, under Major-General William Pulteney, formed by the 4th Division and the 19th Independent Brigade. The 19th Brigade had fought at Mons and the 4th Division at Le Cateau, but only the 19th Brigade had had its full share of marching, and so III Corps was in better shape than the other two. Fatigue would seem to

75

have permeated the BEF, but tiredness is very far from military disaster. All that was needed, as has been seen on so many occasions since, was even a short rest and few hot meals. Morale,except in one or two instances to be seen later,was high and this was appreciated by Sir John French when he visited the troops on the line of march. But fatigue is a deceiver,and can be more dangerous than battle.

Military diseases are infectious, panic being the most virulent of them all. Was it possible that the high proportion of reservists and young soldiers in the BEF, who must have suffered agonies of sore feet, had passed on their malady to their regular long-service comrades? The British Army has made some remarkable marches with seasoned troops, especially in the Peninsular War under appalling conditions. Perhaps with a force composed entirely of serving soldiers the weariness of the BEF might have been far less prominent.

VIII

RETREAT TO THE MARNE
29 AUGUST – 4 SEPTEMBER

In the last chapter it was seen that GHQ, which included Huguet, the French liaison officer, had been plunged in gloom over the supposed outcome of Le Cateau. It was fortunate, however, that when others had lost their heads, Joffre had kept his.

The French Commander-in-Chief had given orders to Lanrezac to counter-attack on the 28th, but Sir John refused to co-operate in this movement with Haig's corps. On the 29th Lanrezac inflicted such a reverse on von Bülow's Second Army at Guise that von Kluck, in answer to his colleague's cry for help, instead of following the Schlieffen Plan, turned in front of Paris, thus compromising, even at this stage, the whole great conception. The Germans inevitably counter-attacked and forced back the corps immediately on the right of I British Corps, thus convincing French that the retreat must continue. This was not to be a controlled withdrawal but a determined rearward move behind the Seine in order that his army might rest and refit. The Channel bases were to be changed to Atlantic ones – St. Nazaire and Le Mans.

So far consideration has only been given to the British right flank. It has been seen that the French troops holding Cambrai, part of 84th Territorial Division, had been forced back during the Battle of Le Cateau to Bapaume. Together with two reserve divisions and Sordet's cavalry they retired on Péronne and thence on Amiens. Just to the south, however, considerable movements were in progress. From the east came the VII Corps which, together with other troops from General Auguste Dubail's First Army in Alsace, Sordet's cavalry, and General d'Amade's two reserve divisions (the Territorials being *hors de combat*), were to form the new Sixth Army under General Michel-Joseph Maunoury at Montdidier. Maunoury was a sixty-seven–year-old wounded veteran of the Franco-Prussian War plucked from retirement, but in Joffre's view 'the complete soldier'. A force was thus gradually being concentrated by rail to cover the British left and to threaten von Kluck's flank.

The Sixth Army was to be constantly reinforced while another new army, the Ninth under General Ferdinand Foch, was being created by a rapid redistribution of the French forces of the centre. A counter-attacking force, as opposed to a covering force, was rapidly taking shape.

In spite of Joffre's supplications French, like Gallio in the New Testament, 'cared for none of these things'; his eyes were fixed on far horizons. The comparison is perhaps hardly fair. What the British Commander-in-Chief did care about was his own army's safety and welfare, although he did not seem to appreciate that, on his own admission, the troops were in no bad shape. GHQ was the Jonah, and its pessimism, combined with the Field-Marshal's distrust of the French, weighed heavily against any co-operation in what he considered to be rash projects.

On the 30th withdrawal continued, and with it came French's definite refusal to Joffre to fill the gap between the Fifth and the newly constituted Sixth Army. The Seine beckoned irresistibly, and thus came about the great Kitchener drama. Kitchener had heard indirectly of what Sir John proposed to do, and so asked him his real intentions. French replied that he was unable to maintain his position in the line and that he proposed to retire behind the Seine, but a further communication from him to the Secretary of State was contradictory: the C-in-C said that he would have liked to attack, and attributed his present situation to the deficiencies in French generalship. The whole basis of this attitude was his deep distrust of the French, begun by his relations with Lanrezac and which now reflected on Joffre. How could the BEF possibly attack when it was unable to defend? It would also seem that the magnitude of the struggle in which he was involved was beyond the British C-in-C's imaginative powers. This was not one of 'Victoria's Little Wars', but already a continental struggle of vast proportions.

By the 31st, in spite of all appeals, Sir John would do nothing except contemplate retreat. But his estimate of II Corps' condition as 'shattered' was ridiculous. He seemed to be obsessed with the word 'refit', and he sent a message to Kitchener the extravagance of which is hard to credit:

If the French go on with their present tactics which are practically to fall back right and left of me, usually without notice, and to abandon all idea of offensive action, of course then the gap in the French Line will remain and the consequence must be borne by them.

As a result of these highly coloured and ambiguous reports Kitchener decided to cross to France. On 1 September he arrived in Paris and met French that afternoon in the British Embassy. The Commander-in-Chief was furious on two counts: first, that the Secretary of State for War wore field-marshal's uniform; and second, that 'K' proposed to visit the troops. The two men, chiefly as the result of Sir Horace Smith-Dorrien's appointment, were not on good terms and these further irritations, as French saw them, only added fuel to the fire. There was neither a valid reason why 'K' should not wear uniform, nor anything wrong in his wish to visit the BEF. A visit, in view of his reputation, would undoubtedly have been a great morale booster. The Ambassador, Sir Francis Bertie, was able to avert the visit, but French harboured deep resentment ever after.

What happened at a private interview after the French politicians had withdrawn is not at all clear, and such as is known unreliable. It is certain that it was concluded that the BEF must remain in the line. How could it possibly do otherwise since the two armies in the northern sector were obviously dependent on each other (although this was sometimes difficult to believe!)?

It is now necessary to return to the front and see what was going on during the absence of the Commander-in-Chief. The British Army crossed the Aisne during the 31st and that night was on a line from south-west of Soissons to the forest of Compiègne.

On 1 September, due to the realignment of the German First Army, it was von Kluck's cavalry that unexpectedly came in touch with the British left. The German horsemen had penetrated through the forest and encountered 1st Cavalry Brigade at Néry. The surprise was mutual but once the British had recovered from the initial confusion due to German shells landing in the horse lines, a famous encounter took place in which 'L' Battery RHA greatly distinguished itself, its one remaining 13-pounder gun firing to the last. British support came from 4th Cavalry and 19th Infantry Brigades, and the Germans, who were equally surprised at the size of the force that they had encountered, lost eight guns and a number of prisoners, which was a very welcome change of circumstances. During this day (1 September) other sharp engagements took place all along the front, but the net result was that for the first time since Le Cateau the BEF was without a gap between its three corps, Sir Douglas Haig's I Corps lying between La Ferté Milon and Betz, Sir Horace Smith-Dorrien's II Corps between Betz and Nanteuil, and Sir William Pulteney's III Corps with the cavalry to the west of Nanteuil.

It is ironic that it was during the absence of the Commander-in-Chief in Paris that the first engagements since Le Cateau should have taken place. His absence, at both Mons and Le Cateau, could not, however, have made a vast difference. Now that reasonably amicable relations had been resumed with the British, Joffre viewed the situation with increasing satisfaction, although that was not shared by the French Government, which left Paris for Bordeaux on the 2nd. A further withdrawal was deemed necessary before the counter-attack against von Kluck's exposed flank could take place. General Joseph-Simon Gallieni, the sixty-five-year-old Military Governor of Paris, now took command of Maunoury's Sixth Army, which by this time was close to the outer defences of the capital.

A further reverse suffered by the French Fifth Army put paid to the fortunes of Lanrezac, who presumably was despatched to Limoges, the final refuge of 'dégommé' French senior officers (thus creating a new word 'Limogé' in the French dictionary in much the same way as did Stellenbosch for British generals during the South African War). Lanrezac was the victim of his own prejudice, anglophobia. The Battle of Guise had been a brilliant counterstroke, and had he been allowed to receive the backing which Haig had been prepared to give him, that action might have become something far more significant than it did. Certainly his anglophobia, in his own eyes, was thus well justified, but he suffered for the common cause. Lanrezac was replaced by his I Corps commander, General Louis Franchet d'Esperey, at fifty-eight an entirely different type of officer, whom the British troops were to nickname 'Desperate Frankey'.

Joffre, as has been seen, had been implementing his plans during these few days by the creation of yet another army in addition to the Sixth, called the Ninth and under the command of Foch. The necessary troops were drawn from the centre, and this force was placed between the Fourth and Fifth Armies to counteract the main German thrust to the south of Rheims. By 4 September Foch was in position to the south of the St. Gond Marshes and centered upon La Fère-Champenoise.

The British had crossed the Marne on 3 September, and still the retreat continued. Both Haig and Smith-Dorrien were worried about the state of their troops, so French spent most of the 4th visiting units and chatting with the men. His capabilities as a morale raiser have always been emphasised, but it was during this further unfortunate absence from his HQ at Melun that two great problems arose. Murray, on the one hand, had agreed to a plan put forward by Gallieni, and Wilson, on the other hand, had agreed to another put forward by Franchet d'Esperey. This latter plan was to be the one adopted by Joffre, but Murray had issued orders on the basis of his meeting with Gallieni which necessitated a further retirement of the BEF, since these orders could not be cancelled.

Sir John once more cared for none of these things and, due to his absence, did not consider himself in any way committed to either plan. Joffre, in so far as was possible for him, shed all his placidity and used every outside means in his power to influence Sir John. Although he had heard that his efforts had been successful, Joffre felt the necessity for a personal appeal and himself went to Melun, where a famous interview took place. Joffre explained his plan and thanked French for his momentous decision. He begged the Commander-in-Chief for the BEF's wholehearted support, since he himself was prepared to sacrifice all in the effort to bring about his great counterstroke: 'Monsieur le Maréchal, c'est la France qui vous supplie'. French, hardly able to speak for his emotion, asked Wilson to translate his own halting words. Wilson, for once laconic, simply said 'The Marshal says yes'.

The gist of Joffre's order was as follows: 'It is necessary to profit by the dangerous situation in which the First German Army has placed itself by concentrating against it the efforts of the Allied Armies on the extreme left. During September 5 all arrangements will be made to begin the attack on the 6th.' The great retreat was over, and a decisive battle was about to begin.

ONE BATTALION'S RETREAT 26 AUGUST-5 SEPTEMBER

During the closing stages of the stand at Le Cateau, away on the left flank, the 4th Division had retired south-west on the village of Vendhuille, not without some confusion and loss. The 1st King's Own Regiment of 12th Brigade and part of the 1st Royal Warwickshire Regiment of 10th Brigade did not receive orders to withdraw and so held on until late into the night of the 26th when, almost surrounded, they successfully fought their way out. The rest of 12th Brigade was not seriously molested in its retirement. Although they did not reach Vendhuille, on the Escaut, until 10.30 p.m. after four hours' marching, the Essex were on the march again at 3 a.m. on the 27th, several officers who were sleeping in a barn only narrowly escaping being left behind.

The 12th Brigade was divisional rearguard and when the Essex marched through Ronssoy to the south end of that village, they took up a position at Râperie together with the 2nd Royal Inniskilling Fusiliers to cover the retirement. An Essex officer recorded:

> It was a most extraordinary feeling to watch from a post on a slope of a hill, which recalled Portsdown Hills at Portsmouth, the seemingly interminable procession of ambulances, wagons, artillery, machine-gun teams and infantry units all moving away from the sound of the guns, which crept nearer and nearer, for the cavalry were falling back before the German advance. It was a stern test of discipline for the men for they must have realised that should the enemy break in they were expected to guarantee with their lives the safety of the Division. We settled down as best we could with the knowledge that each hour brought the Germans nearer and that the incessant gunfire might break in earnest over our heads again.

The enemy did not immediately press the pursuit and, the main body having passed through, orders came to fall back and occupy a further position one mile south of Templeau-le-Guezard, a high point on a river called, ironically, the Cologne (tributary to the Somme) commanding the road northward. Some hours passed and the Battalion again retired, this time via Hervilly to Hancourt, which was reached after a two-hour   march at 5.30

82

p.m. on the 27th. At this village 'A', 'B' and 'C' Companies were detailed for outpost duty, but the Essex were to know no rest for at 10.30 p.m. they were on the move again in a twelve-hour march, this time for Sancourt, ten miles away near the north bank of the Somme. Having been marching and fighting since 2 a.m. on the 25th the infantry of 4th Division were thoroughly tired out, and artillery limbers, baggage vehicles, and carts of all descriptions were used to to ease their feet.

When the Somme was reached at Voyennes orders came for all impedimenta to be offloaded, and officers and men to be carried instead to the full capacity of transport, both horse and mechanical. This instruction was strictly obeyed, with the result that officers lost their entire kits and many men were without waterproof sheets for a month. Sancourt was entered at 10 a.m. on 28 August. The Battalion had then been on the march continuously since it left Vendhuille at 3 a.m. on the 27th, a period of thirty-one hours, during which time it had covered over twenty miles.

Sancourt was evacuated without resistance. The Essex moved off at 2 p.m. as advance-guard to the Brigade and were soon near Ham, with the Germans at the heels of II Corps. At 10.30 p.m. the wearied men bivouacked at Campagne on the River Meve. On the 29th the enemy pursuit slackened and the whole of the British Army rested, the Essex forming the rearguard of the Brigade during the day's respite.

A 9 p.m. the withdrawal was resumed in the direction of Noyon. For most of the 1914-18 war this was the nearest occupied town to Paris, which unpleasant fact Georges 'The Tiger' Clemenceau, the Prime Minister of France for the war's final crucial year, was constantly to remind his compatriots with the ominous words '*Les Allemands sont à Noyon*'. In the early morning of 30 August 10th Brigade became rearguard and, with the rest of 12th Brigade, marching all day, the Battalion bivouacked in the streets of Breuil at 10 p.m. Still moving southwards, the Essex left the village at 7 a.m. on the 31st and reached the Forest of Compiègne, one of the most beautiful woodlands in the north of France and where two armistices were to be signed, one in 1918 and the other, with Hitler present, in 1940. By the Paris road the Battalion reached Verberie at 10 p.m. and bivouacked.

At 7 a.m. on 1 September the Pompadours went across country

to Ducy Baron and there covered the retirement of the rest of the Brigade, while from the east and north-east came the sound of a heavy engagement. This was the fight at Néry and the famous stand of 'L' Battery RHA, which enabled the 1st Middlesex Regiment to restore the situation after the 1st Cavalry Brigade had been surprised by equally surprised Germans. Although not engaged, the 4th Division did not withdraw further that day.

At 2.25 a.m. on 2 September the retreat was continued to Lagny on the Marne. There was little movement on the 3rd, for the long march was nearly at its end. At 8.30 p.m., after a short march, the Battalion reached Ferrières and rested for the night in the park owned by the Baron de Rothschild. A very muddy and dirty private soldier in French uniform came up to the CO and said that dinner would be served to the officers in the Château. This proved to be the Baron himself – what he was doing at home and at the same time in uniform history does not relate.

During this respite an officer wrote 'There must have been an impression that things were going right as all night long battalion were passing on the road not singing "Tipperary" but "A little grey home in the West". This shows how greatly the Germans erred when they thought the long retreat had shaken the morale of the British soldier.'

In the early morning of 5 September the march was resumed as far as Brie-Comte-Robert, where the welcome news was received of the end of the retreat.

IX

THE 'MIRACLE' OF THE MARNE'
5-9 SEPTEMBER

Sir Edward Creasy in his *The Fifteen Decisive Battles of the World*, first published in 1851, defines such a battle as one in which, had the result gone the other way, the course of history would have been equally changed. Was the Battle of the Marne a decisive battle? The answer is that it was, although it must have been one of the least bloody and most protracted of such battles, being more a series of engagements of varying intensity and distances apart. Had the Germans captured Paris and the Channel Ports there is small doubt as to what the result would have been. Since they failed in these objectives, they had in effect lost the war, although this remarkable fact was probably not appreciated at the time by either side. Whatever the outcome, German victory on the Marne would have changed history; the whole question will be considered later together with the situation that led to the fall of France in 1940.

The circumstances which brought about the so-called 'Miracle of the Marne' must now be examined in more detail, and from the strategic, rather than the more limited tactical, viewpoints of the northern armies.

In the first place it has been shown that Joffre, following the trend of French military thought, had formed as large a reserve as possible, in order to manoeuvre either in attack or defence according to the exigencies of the day-to-day situation.

Not content therefore with the formation of the Sixth Army, he had on 29 August ordered the formation of a Ninth Army under Foch. This army was largely drawn from the Fourth, which had been the least tried of all the French forces. Ninth Army was positioned between the Fourth and Fifth Armies so that the Fifth Army, by moving to its left, might be more effectively used in the counterstroke against von Kluck. By 4 September Foch had, as has already been briefly noted, taken up a position to the south of the St Gond Marshes and centered on La Fère-Champenoise. That day Joffre issued the famous order quoted in the previous chapter.

The objectives of the different armies were given as follows: Maunoury with the Sixth Army was to attack eastwards with the object of driving the Germans over the Ourcq; the British Army was to change front to the east, with its left on Coulommiers, and attack towards Montmirail while the Fifth Army advanced due north. Farther to the right, Foch was to hold the weight of the enemy in the centre of the new front and so cover the offensive of the Fifth Army. In brief, this was the order that turned retreat into advance and changed the whole course of the war in the west.

The part to be played by the BEF, as originally intended, must be understood because it has been suggested that Maunoury was not given enough support. The British line of advance was originally north-east between the Fifth and Sixth Armies with the object of attacking von Kluck's flank south of the Marne, while Franchet d'Esperey attacked his front. It was not until 7 September that Joffre, more certainly informed of the German movements, requested a move farther to the north. No request was made originally for the BEF to aid Maunoury on the Ourcq.

As to the the German point of view, it would appear that even on the day previous to the advance they thought that the Allied left had been beaten, and that the right was still the strongest part of the whole French line. Troops from the right wing had of course been used to create the two new armies. It was due to a hard-fought defensive action at Nancy by General Edouard de Castelnau's Second Army that not only were the Kaiser's hopes of making an entry into that city frustrated, but the great counterstroke was also aided, for von Kluck, ignorant of Maunoury's strength and of the defeat before Nancy, continued to commit himself southwards.

On the evening of the 5th, von Kluck received bad news, first of the failure of the attack on Nancy, and then of the strengthening of the French left. Suddenly he became aware that Maunoury was a serious threat to his rear.

That same afternoon of the 5th, in contrast to the alarm and despondency in the German camp, there was joy and thankfulness in the British, since it was then that the orders came to about-face. There

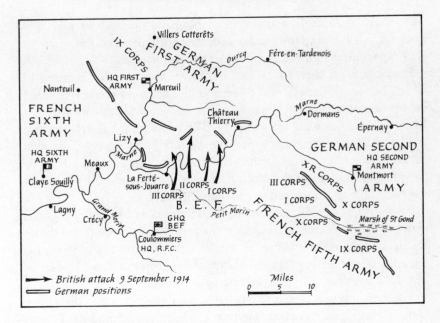

The Battle of the Marne, 5-9 September 1914

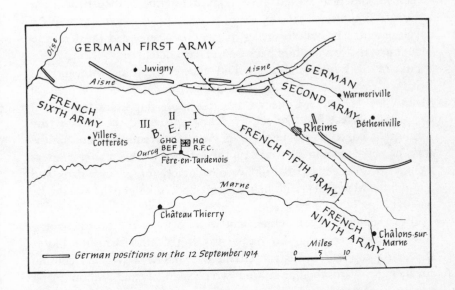

The Battle of the Aisne, 12-20 September 1914

were still considerable deficiences to be made up both in men and material, but the fillip to morale, with the continuing good weather, at once compensated for the earlier trials and tribulations.

It would seem that von Kluck's plan, in view of the situation in which he found himself, was to reassemble, behind a screen provided by his reserve corps, a large force to destroy Maunoury; von der Marwitz's cavalry was to hold up the BEF while his left, in conjunction with von Bülow's right, stopped the French Fifth Army. This plan completely miscarried since the BEF and the Fifth Army both made progress, but farther to the south Foch was being attacked heavily and the Ninth Army was forced to give some ground.

By the night of 5 September the Germans realised that their overall plan had failed. Nancy had not fallen, a personal disappointment to the Kaiser, and the right was not, as was thought even up to this moment, pursuing a beaten enemy; this latter misconception can be seen as being the basis for the whole German plan's failure.

Another plan was therefore needed to overwhelm Foch in the centre and for von Kluck to defeat Maunoury, while the BEF and the French Fifth Army were held in check by comparatively weak forces. If successful, this plan would once again defeat the Franco-British left wing and capture Paris. In short, frontal attacks were to replace envelopment. The whole success of the plan depended on defeating Maunoury and driving him back on the Paris defences.

First of all, however, Foch would have to be dealt with, and the British Army held off long enough for the complete eclipse of Maunoury. The second essential was the more important, for even if the plan to defeat Foch failed von Kluck, provided the Sixth Army was liquidated, could escape the trap. And, with reinforcements on the way, he could once more attack on the extreme left even after so great a delay. If, however, the British were to attack von Kluck's flank and rear while Maunoury still held his ground, then retreat would be inevitable.

On 6 September von Kluck sent two corps to the north, having taken a hasty decision. So hasty was it that the British I Corps, advancing towards the River Grand Morin, saw a German column advancing towards them, a column which suddenly and without firing a shot turned north.

The British supposed that the enemy were in full retreat, but this was not yet to be; all they were doing was altering their dispositions. On the front of the BEF only part of von der Marwitz's cavalry and their support group were left to act as rearguard, but the German cavalry, not trained to fight on foot, were unable to delay the British advance as von Kluck had hoped. Time to crush Maunoury, whose army was daily increasing in strength, was therefore running out.

The position now was that, since Maunoury was able to hold his own, the British and French Fifth Armies moved steadily northward while, in the centre, Foch, hard pressed but counter-attacking whenever possible, was slowly being pushed back. The critical day was 8 September. Maunoury was forced back owing to the exhaustion of his troops and further deployment by von Kluck on his northern flank. The Germans reached the outskirts of Meaux.

It was at this point that, in addition to other reinforcements, Gallieni's much-publicised evening sortie from Paris of 6000 men of IV Corps, in two lifts by 600 taxis and motor-buses, took place. Each taxi carried five or six men to the front, covering thirty-seven miles in the round trip. This new departure in military transport, indeed history's first lorried infantry, rather naturally caught the public imagination. Coulommiers was entered by the BEF on the 7th after a hasty retreat by the Germans. The enemy, as was their habit, had thoroughly pillaged the little town, smashing what they could not carry away.

On the 8th the day ended after some fairly stiff fighting with both the British and the French Fifth Army across the Petit Morin river, having taken several hundred prisoners and some guns. These successes gave a further boost to the advance – now it was the Germans who provided souvenirs in the shape of helmets and even greatcoats to a once-more exuberant BEF.

Fortunately for the advance, von Kluck's orders to blow the Marne bridges came too late, except for those at La Ferté-sous-Jouarre, so on the 9th, in spite of very favourable positions, the enemy made no attempt to defend that part of the Marne valley to the west of Château-Thierry. By the morning of the 9th Smith-Dorrien's II Corps had crossed the Marne and the leading brigade of 3rd Division was four miles beyond the river.

It was now that there occurred an unfortunate hold-up. Had the whole line been able to press forward, a considerable part of the German First Army might have been cut off. As it was, Haig's I Corps on the right was delayed by the threat of a flank attack from the direction of Château-Thierry, still held by the Germans, and could not advance until the afternoon. Pulteney's III Corps on the left, unable to cross the Marne at La Ferté-sous-Jouarre, where the bridges had been destroyed, was held up by a strong German rearguard action on the line Château-Thierry–Lizy.

The situation along the whole front was critical. Von Kluck made one last effort to defeat Maunoury, but the Germans were nearing exhaustion, and were short of both food and ammunition, since their lines of communication were hampered because the forts of Maubeuge were still holding out. The British were, however, across the Marne, and in order to meet this threat von Kluck had to reinforce his left. What was to follow was far more serious: because of the British advance, von Bülow was retreating.

There now follows one of the most extraordinary happenings in a time of extraordinary happenings, no less a phenomenon than a lieutenant-colonel giving positive orders to three army commanders Lieutenant-Colonel Hentsch, von Moltke's Chief of Intelligence and a confirmed pessimist, because of great delays in all communications systems, was sent by car from Luxembourg to the three right-wing headquarters with full powers.

Owing to von Kluck's depredations to increase his pressure on Maunoury, the right of von Bülow's Second Army position had become exceedingly dangerous, full advantage of which was being taken by Franchet d'Esperey. The French Fifth Army Commander had been so successful that he was able to send help to Foch, suffering heavy attacks from both von Bülow's left and von Hausen's Third Army. Hentsch arrived at Bülow's HQ just when the latter was greatly worried by Franchet d'Esperey's defeat of his right and the gap left by von Kluck's reinforcements to fight Maunoury. Into this gap the British were also advancing to the Marne, west of Château-Thierry. Von Bülow and Hentsch decided between them that the only course left open was a general retreat to the Aisne. Hentsch therefore went off to von Kluck's HQ to force him to do just this.

The result was complete anti-climax, for when Foch, who had been fighting his defensive battle, was at last ready to attack, the great, much-advertised counterstroke in the St Gond Marshes hit air, the Germans having already retired. So much then for 'Miracle of the

Marne'. It was not the attack, but Foch's magnificent defence, which constituted the miracle at that point. Legend made him say on 8 September *'Ma droite est enforcée, ma gauche cède, tout va bien. J'attaque!'* ('My right is driven back, my left is giving way, situation excellent. I attack!'). Unfortunately, *l'attaque* never came, but this anti-climax in no way detracts from the great defence put up by Foch and his Ninth Army, though unnecessary casualties were caused by fruitless counter-attacks.

Praise is also due to Maunoury for his fight using a heterogeneous force that arrived piecemeal on the battlefield, often by means of unorthodox transport; and inspired and inspected by Gallieni, the Governor of Paris.

It was, however, Joffre the unflappable, by his patience and flair for the right moment to strike, who had turned the tide of the German flood which, defeated by minds too full of false ideas about their enemies, thus lost all hopes of a quick victory. So much for the French. Credit must be given to them for rethinking in the face of the circumstances their own preconceived ideas, as embodied in Plan XVII, and putting up two such notable defensive actions.

But what of the British? The about-turn had had far-reaching effects on morale, and must have provided wonderful opportunities for initiative, even down to company level. (Compared with what was to follow , however, minor tactics were of small importance, especially in view of the static warfare that was to set in almost immediately.) Is it too much to say that it was the British Army that turned the scale against von Kluck?

Von Bülow wrote in his account of the Battle of the Marne:

As the enemy crossed the Marne in several columns, between La Ferté'-sous-Jouarre and Château-Thierry, early on the morning of 9 September, there could be no doubt but that the tactical and general situation made the retreat of the First Army necessary, and that the Second Army must also retreat if its right flank was not to be completely enveloped.

When the British Army crossed the Marne on the morning of 9 September the French Sixth Army was almost at the end of its endurance, and it is evident that no troops placed on the defensive as were Maunoury's can force an enemy to retire. The French Fifth

Army did not cross the Marne until the *evening* of the 9th, which can hardly have affected the operations of the morning. It was surely the British threat to his flank that precipitated von Bülow's decision to retreat, and which also saved Maunoury in his so-dangerous situation.

There have been many criticisms levelled at the slowness of the BEF advance. Two corps were taken away by von Kluck from the line of British movement to reinforce his offensive against Maunoury, and it is often suggested that he was only able to do this because of the slow khaki advance.

It has already been shown that Joffre had wished to draw back his left still farther in order to be able more effectively to attack von Kluck's flank, and on 3 September French had received a request to move his armies back to the Seine. By the morning of 5 September the BEF, after a night march, was fifteen miles south-west of Coulommiers. Von Kluck was aware of his danger only on the evening of that day and on the 6th began his march northward. The BEF, given this problem of time and distance, could not have prevented this movement.

On 9 September, it will be remembered, only II Corps was able to cross the Marne. Although well in advance of the French Fifth Army, I Corps was delayed by a movement from the east, and III Corps was delayed by the destroyed bridges. There were presumed to be strong German forces coming from the right and, if they had caught the BEF crossing the river, the result might have been disastrous.

Von Bülow's decision to retreat could not have been known, nor could the fact that the 'strong forces' were a cavalry screen to mask the withdrawal. Consequently, in the light of what was known at the time, it would have been folly to attempt a dangerous river crossing.

With hindsight, criticism is easy. It is not the might-have-been that is important, but what is actually accomplished under the known circumstances. After all the vicissitudes it had been through, from top to bottom, it is possible that it was the much-tried BEF which had really performed the 'Miracle of the Marne'.

ONE BATTALION'S MARNE 5-9 SEPTEMBER

On 5 September the British Army, lying between the French

Sixth Army on the left and the Fifth on the right, was behind the Grand Morin, occupying the line Bailly-La Houssay-Courpalay, Pulteney's III Corps (4th Division and 19th Brigade) being concentrated about Bailly. On the morning of the 6th, amid much cheering, the BEF changed front.

At 7.48 p.m. on 5 September, the 4th Division received orders that the British Army was about to take the offensive north-eastwards against the German right flank in conjunction with the French Sixth Army, the Germans having moved south-east against the French Fifth Army. III Corps was to advance towards Serris, II Corps being on its right. The 4th Division was ordered to provide an advance guard of an infantry brigade (10th) and attached troops, and a left flank guard of two battalions (2000 men) and one battery (6 guns) on reaching Ferrières.

The instructions to the advance guard were not to go beyond Serris, but on arrival there they were to throw out a screen to cover the rest of 4th Division's advance, and to reconnoitre as far as they could with the cyclist company, in an effort to make contact with the enemy. The division started the forward movement at 3 a.m. on the morning of 6 September. By 5 a.m. the divisional cyclists reported that the roads were clear for a mile round Serris and the GOC ordered the occupation of Bailly. It was then determined to assemble 4th Division in and about Jossigny, under cover of the advance guard at Serris and Bailly. The left flank guard was withdrawn to the latter place while 10th and 12th Brigades were instructed to prepare for an advance on the plateau to the north-east about Magny and Romainvilliers, while 11th Brigade established an observation line along Villiers-Coupuray and made contact with II Corps.

At 2 p.m. 4th Division HQ (82 men, 54 horses) was at Villeneuve-le-Comte, when information came that I Corps were engaged near Rozay. II Corps therefore moved south-east in support and III Corps inclined east in co-operation; the special duty of 4th Division being to observe the valley of the Grand Morin and to provide against attack from the north-east.

At 7.40 p.m. the 12th Brigade commander was ordered to reconnoitre the bridges over the Grand Morin, orders having come that the pursuit of the enemy was to be pressed (*sic*). At 11 a.m. on the 7th the Essex were advance guard to the Brigade. Near the village of La Haute Maison, where they bivouacked, they surprised a patrol of about 20 Uhlans, who hastily retired. The Battalion, although under occasional infantry fire, suffered no casualties during the day.

The Essex moved off at 6.30 a.m. on 8 September, and orders were received to seize the high ground from which they could cover the artillery shelling the enemy crossing the Marne at La Ferté. The Essex and the 2nd Royal Inniskillings Fusiliers there pressed on to the river and met with some enemy resistance. This day was of considerable importance as more orders were received to push forward as quickly as possible – all along the roads the relics of the hurried German retreat could be seen.

Yet 9 September was even more profitable than the previous day, for during daylight hours the Marne was crossed by a notable feat of arms. The 11th Brigade had been unable to cross the broken bridges at La Ferté owing to snipers and machine-gun fire. There was not enough bridging material to span the Marne which at this point was both broad and deep. In order to turn the enemy's flank the Battalion was ordered to choose a point on the right to cross the river; the Essex CO also had under command the 2nd Lancashire Fusiliers.

It was decided to make the attempt at a lock lying to the west of Luzancy. 'D' Company acted as advance guard and moved through the woods to within half a mile of the lock. Here the men were halted and the Company Commander and a subaltern went forward to reconnoitre, being joined shortly afterwards by the brigade machine-gun officer, they found a concealed line of approach and a position for the machine-guns. The Company was then guided to the edge of the woods within 400 yards of the objective. In front was the roadway, then the watermeadows and causeway leading to the lock-keeper's house. The Marne lay beyond, with, on the far bank, the village of Chamigny.

The question was whether that village was held in force, or whether the enemy were still withdrawing. (A small diversion was started by a white spaniel running about looking for rabbits.) It was agreed that if the position was occupied the enemy must be in a small copse on the bank opposite the lock gates. This surmise proved right, since later a body of Germans was observed hurrying across the open country to the rear, while a continual stream of horsemen and wagons was seen retiring along the tree-lined highway, clearly outlined on the skyline. A small party was detailed to make a dash from the woods, cross the road and, under cover of some dead ground, reach the riverbank. As they ran down the slope the enemy opened fire from the opposite bank, receiving an instant reply from the machine-guns. With this covering fire the little party reached the bank, having had two casualties. They had, however, found a covered way and, guided by a private soldier, two platoons or half the company, 106 men, were able to reinforce the small group.

The lock-keeper's house, a square two-storeyed building overlooking the enemy's position, appeared to be locked and unoccupied, but the door was suddenly opened by the lock-keeper and his wife, who were in sole possession. All was now ready for the crossing; and a strong party lined the bank to cover the passage of the river. The Company Commander ran forward and crossed by the narrow railed footbridge that ran along the top of the lock gates. Some of the planks had been removed but he clambered over by the girders and luckily found only a dead German in possession on the far side, the others having fled. 'D' Company crossed rapidly and, extending outwards, formed a bridgehead, under cover of which the remainder of the Battalion crossed, followed by the Lancashire Fusiliers and the 1st Battalion The Rifle Brigade.

X

THE AISNE AND THE 'RACE TO THE SEA' 10 SEPTEMBER – 10 OCTOBER

General Maxime Weygand, Foch's famous chief of staff, denied that the words quoted in the last chapter were ever spoken by his chief. Be that as it may, those words, and the man who supposedly uttered them, have gone down in history as the inspiration of the 'miracle'. Inspiration Foch may have been, but it was the BEF which supplied the loaves and fishes.

Both sides were exhausted. The Germans, to drown their sorrows in defeat did so literally with drunkenness and wanton pillage; and many officers and soldiers too drunk to continue the rearward march added considerably to the BEF total of 5000 prisoners and twenty guns. Had the French been capable of a more rapid pursuit the Crown Prince of Saxony and his staff, lunching too well in Châlons, might have been added to the bag. But by now the Ninth Army, in spite of Foch's exhortations, was incapable of speed, being worn down by the casualties suffered in the costly counter-attacks across the St. Gond Marshes, country ideally suited for defence.

The weather had broken, which naturally delayed the advance, as also did the timely arrival of German reinforcements, and by 14 September the Allied armies reached the line of the River Aisne. On this day also the unfortunate von Moltke, the arbiter of defeat, was replaced by the fifty-two-year-old Prussian War Minister, General Erich von Falkenhayn. Poor Moltke, he was the victim of his own virtues, modesty, an attractive manner, and intellectual gifts that were a positive disadvantage in his exalted position. Unable to make decisions, he was at the mercy of his subordinate commanders who were, in the right wing of the army, at loggerheads with each other. From this disastrous *contretemps* sprang the whole failure of the

British and French staff officers, 1914.
Left to right: Haig (I Corps); Joffre (C–in–C
French forces); Smith-Dorrien (II Corps);
French (C–in–C BEF); de Castelnau (French
Second Army); Pau. Colour lithograph after
an oil painting by Septimeus E. Scott – the
artist has almost caricatured the popular
notion of French excitability and British
phlegm.

The old and the new: Lords Haldane (left)
and Kitchener at the War Office. Kitchener
succeeded Asquith as Minister of War on
5 August 1914.

F-M Sir Henry Wilson, 'An Ulsterman of
much shrewdness and charm, as well as a
born intriguer' (engraving by John Day).
As Director of Military Operations, he did
much to foster good relations between the
British and French, but 'he got into a state
of sexual excitement whenever he saw a
politician'.

Haig, French's chief detractor and his successor as C-in-C in 1915, 'one of those soldiers who have difficulty in ingratiating themselves with the lower ranks'. From a lithograph after a painting by Sir James Guthrie.

Col-Gen Alexander von Kluck, C-in-C German First Army; 'he may not have been a great general, but he was a brave old man'.

Left: 'The Man Who Disobeyed', Lt-Gen Sir Horace Smith-Dorrien, from a 'Spy' cartoon. 'Like many others, he paid the penalty for being right', and for falling foul of French.

Right: The 'War Lord', Kaiser Wilhelm II (left) with the Chief of the German General Staff, General Helmuth von Moltke. Von Moltke, 'a victim of his own defects', probably ensured by his plan that Germany would lose the war.

'By efficient organisation, the Regular Army mobilisation which had begun in the afternoon of 4 August was followed by embarkation only five days later'. The 1st Leicesters going aboard a troopship at Southampton.

Although the gallant Belgian defence of Liège delayed von Kluck for two days at most, those days were vital to the BEF. The city fell on 16 August.

Although thought by many to be 'of no military value', aircraft, despite their crudity and lack of armament, proved to be essential for reconnaissance. 3 Squadron, RFC on a scratch airfield near Amiens in 1914: the first machine is a Blériot monoplane, almost identical to that in which Louis Blériot flew the Channel in 1909.

'The first time a British army had met a continental enemy for nearly 100 years' – British troops in Mons, before the battle, 22 August. The slagheaps that characterise 'this unlovely mining country' can be clearly seen.

'A battle that should never have been fought' – Mons, 23 August. The defence of Jemappes Bridge on the Mons/Condé Canal by the 1st Royal Scots Fusiliers, from a coloured lithograph after a painting by Gilbert Holiday.

Le Cateau – 'an encounter between nineteenth-century minds and twentieth-century weapons'. Captain Reynolds saving the guns of 37 Battery, RFA, in action on 26 August, for which feat he was awarded the Victoria Cross. From a painting by W. B. Wollen.

Above: In October the war began to change. Since neither side could beat or outflank the other, the armies started to dig, a situation that would continue for more than 3½ years. British troops in a communications trench (crude by later standards) at the beginning of a battle whose name would become synonymous with the whole war – Ypres.

Left: No trenches, no mud, no shell-holes, no wire – the first months of the Great War were fought in open country, and were characterised by considerable mobility. French and German dead after a charge near Epernay, during the 'Miracle of the Marne', September 1914.

Right: First Ypres – 'the grave of the old Regular Army'. Searching for snipers from an early British trench, November 1914.

Above: The Germans were much hampered by the deliberate flooding of the Yser valley between Nieuport and Dixmude. The Belgian defence, inspired by King Albert, combined with these floods, secured the Allied flank from all attempts to turn it.

The Indian Corps remained in France until the end of 1915, suffering severely under the appalling conditions. Gurkha infantrymen (below) and Indian machine-gunners (right) in France at the time of First Ypres.

German infantry with a machine-gun team in a front-line trench during First Ypres, November 1914. By now, a static war was inevitable.

'One of the most brilliant feats of arms from a single battalion in the 1914–18 war, perhaps ever' – the 2nd Worcesters' famous charge against the Prussian Guard at Gheluvelt, 31 October (from a painting by F. Matania). But for the Worcesters, the Germans might have penetrated and then turned the whole Allied line round Ypres.

'None but the brave?' – a fantasy of 1914. Perceptions of the war in Britain did not match the harsh reality of the fighting, while 'German atrocity' stories were increasingly popular with newspaper readers. The Munster Fusiliers rescuing the nuns of Ypres, December 1914.

Schlieffen Plan and the situation in which the Germans now found themselves, dug in along the line of the Aisne in good defensive positions. From these positions the Allies could not shift them, a stalemate which was to last for four years.

Both sides were thus literally bogged down. In spite of strong attacks by both the French and British no progress was made, and it was clear that the only solution to the problem was a move round the right flank of the enemy, and possibly the relief of the Belgians in Antwerp. The Germans had a similar idea, with the capture of the Channel ports as their objective. Thus began the so-called 'Race to the Sea'.

Sir John French, it must be admitted, was not slow to see the alternatives, the one being an entrenched warfare of attrition, the other the necessity of defending the Channel ports. He realised in the first instance that the predominance of the artillery made trenches an essential protection, and in the second that, if the Channel ports were to be saved, it was the BEF which should save them, and at the same time shorten its lines of communication with England.

A further division, the 6th, had by this time arrived from England and had been absorbed into III Corps. The ebb and flow of the tide of battle along the Aisne, in deplorable weather, convinced French, ably abetted by Henry Wilson, that the move involved in his second alternative must be made.

On 27 September therefore, Sir John made overtures to Joffre regarding the transference of the BEF from the Aisne to the left of the Allied line covering the Channel ports. Joffre agreed to this proposal in principle, provided that adequate transport arrangements could be made such as would not hinder the movement of French reinforcements. The result of these negotiations was that the British II and III Corps were transferred to the sector between Béthune and Ypres by 9-12 October, II Corps being moved as far as St. Pol partly by about 400 motor-buses borrowed from the French. I Corps then arrived on 20 October and took over the northern sector of the Ypres front. Sir John moved his GHQ to Abbeville on 8 October, and on his way met Foch at Doullens, as did the inevitable Wilson, much to the mutual delight of the two old friends. This meeting created a far better feeling between the Allies. Wilson's friendship with Foch, now the co-ordinator of the northern group of armies, had considerable influence on Sir John, who was ever suspicious of French intentions.

Crisis was not far away, however. On 28 September the heavy Austrian 305mm Skoda howitzers, which had reduced the fortresses of Liège and Namur, started the bombardment of Antwerp, to which the Belgian field army had retired after the fall of the other two fortresses. Antwerp, with a circumference of sixty-two miles of fortifications similar to those of Liège and Namur, was consequently unable to withstand bombardment and capitulated on 10 October.

Before Antwerp capitulated, there had been much heartsearching by the British Government about whether or not to organise a force to relieve the Belgian city. The result was that, largely owing to Winston Churchill (who for the occasion donned the uniform, *faute de mieux*, of an Elder Brother of Trinity House), a strange expedition was mounted. This consisted mainly of a naval division that was completely untrained and which, having landed at Dunkirk, reached Antwerp on 4 October. Some of these unfortunates later made an escape, including such famous names as Rupert Brooke and Bernard Freyberg, but many, losing their way, crossed over into Holland and were interned for the rest of the war.

A more substantial contribution was made by the War Office in the shape of IV Corps (the 7th Division and 3rd Cavalry Division) commanded by Major-General Sir Henry Rawlinson. This contingent landed at Ostend and Zeebrugge during 6-8 October, but of course too late to affect the situation.

Antwerp capitulated on 10 October, the Belgian forces having been withdrawn and positioned behind the Scheldt, and later placed on the line of the River Yser from Dixmude to the sea at Nieuport. This withdrawal was covered by Rawlinson's force and a French Marine brigade under Rear-Admiral Ronarc'h. Once the Belgian Army was secure behind the Yser, Rawlinson's Corps came under the command of Sir John French, who had reacted rather petulantly to this independent command, in which he suspected the hand of Kitchener.

As has been said, French met Foch at Doullens, the latter now effectively in control of the whole northern sector. In such a position he was Joffre's deputy, a position which some thought should have gone to Gallieni, still Military Governor of Paris, and who was in fact senior to both Joffre and Foch. Gallieni was another popular candidate for 'miracle-worker of the Marne', probably due to his timely use of the Paris transport services to reinforce Maunoury, but Joffre, while being jealous of Gallieni, had complete confidence in Foch.

There was at this time no real question of a unified command. Foch could only convey Joffre's wishes to French, but fortunately, due to the rapport with Wilson, this was made much easier than might have been expected. In addition, Sir John himself had a good opinion of Foch, and shared his views regarding a movement round the still-open flank.

On 13 October British GHQ moved to St Omer, but in spite of pressure from this quarter no great progress was made by the BEF, and any idea of a positive offensive movement was quickly dispelled by the surprise appearance of the German Fourth Army. This was newly constituted by the raising of four reserve corps, seventy-five per cent consisting of untrained but enthusiastic recruits obtained from the higher educational establishments. Lack of training was to be compensated for by a greater provision of heavy artillery.

As early as 10 October the Army Commander, Duke Albrecht of Würtemberg, had received the following order from von Falkenhayn at his HQ, now at Charleville-Mézières:

'The new Fourth Army will advance, regardless of losses, with its right flank on the sea coast in order to cut off the fortresses of Dunkirk and Calais. These will be captured later and then will swing southward leaving St Omer on its left.'

Both sides were therefore always thinking of enveloping movements. The plans were to fail – instead the two armies met head on and produced what the British were to call 'First Ypres'.

ONE BATTALION'S CROSSING OF THE AISNE – 12 SEPTEMBER – 6 OCTOBER

The First Battle of the Aisne, which marked the last stage of the campaign of the Marne, embraced an attempt by the Allied left to push the German right from the positions north of the river, and thus to keep in being the war of movement. The operation was one of the most difficult for troops to execute, for a full river, some 170ft broad and 15ft deep in the centre, had first to be crossed under observed artillery fire. Then the heights beyond had to be seized and maintained against obstinate opposition. The Official History comments that 'The actual passage of the Aisne is likely to be remembered in the annals of the Army as a very remarkable feat, consisting, as it did, of forcing a passage frontally without possibility of manoeuvre.'

To quote John Buchan's *A History of the Great War*:

The German armies had chosen for their stand, not the line of the Aisne, but the crest of the plateau beyond it, at an average of two miles from the stream side. The place had once been used before as a defensive position by an invader – by Blücher in February and March 1814 – and the study of that campaign may have suggested the idea to the German Staff. A more perfect position could not be found. It commanded all the crossings of the river and most of the roads on the south bank, and even if the Allies reached the north side the outjutting spurs gave excellent opportunities for an enfilading fire. The blindness of the crests made it almost impossible for the German trenches to be detected.

On the evening of 12 September III Corps (still composed of 4th Division and 19th Brigade) was on the British left in the neighbourhood of Buzancy, just to the south of Soissons, with II Corps in the centre, I Corps on the right, and Maunoury's French Sixth Army moving on Soissons. The next day, the 13th, the bulk of the British Army crossed the Aisne to the east of the famous French town, doing so with the river in flood and in heavy rain. The 4th Division went over at Venizel, on the main road from Soissons to Rheims, by means of a partially destroyed road bridge. II Corps had much hard fighting before it took up positions with its left resting in the village of Ste Marguerite, part of 5th Division having to be ferried across on rafts. I Corps also had a difficult passage, but ultimately made good at Passy, Moulins and Vendresse. When night fell only six infantry brigades of the British Army were left on the south bank, including 19th Brigade of III Corps.

The forward effort was continued and the 4th Division endeavoured to win the uplands of Bucy-le-Long, lying between Vrégny and Chivres, from the German II Corps, but was stayed by artillery fire. On the British right I Corps effected a lodgement on the plateau in the neighbourhood of Troyon and Chivy, but by the 15th heavy enemy reinforcements caused a reaction. The

4th Division had difficulty in maintaining the ground south of Vrégny, and the same problem faced the 5th Division near Chivres and Condé. There was still hope that the Chemin des Dames would ultimately fall to the Allies, but though a gallant movement by the French Sixth Army eased the anxiety of 4th Division, the French on the right had to give ground, and by 18 September both forces were digging in. The famous highway remained in German hands – a constant menace to the Allies.

The greater part of 10 September was occupied in passing 4th Division over the repaired bridges at La Ferté and the Saussoy railway bridge. The 12th Brigade was advance guard and as part of this force, at 9 a.m. on the 10th, the 2nd Essex marched to the road junction at Les Davids and halted until 1 p.m. Then, by the main road, the Battalion passed through Dhuisy, Coulombs, Hervilliers, Cerfroid, throwing out an outpost line along the road from the last-named place to Brumetz, where many signs of the enemy's hasty retirement were found. Leaving its bivouac at 5 a.m. on the 11th, the Battalion halted for two hours at Cerfroid, and again at Montigny for one hour. Noroy was reached via Mareuil-sur-Ourcq, St. Quentin-Louvry and Passy, and the men were in billets at 7.30. They were early on the move on the 12th, for at 3 a.m. they were marching past Carrière to L'Evêque, and it was 6.30 p.m. before rest was found in a cave upon a farm, there being some anxiety lest the straw on which the men lay might catch fire and thus lead to a terrible disaster. The officers managed to obtain shelter from the heavy rain on a veranda, but their rest was frequently disturbed by other units trying to obtain a footing there.

On 13 September, in pouring rain, the Battalion crossed the Aisne. It left the bivouac at 7 a.m., the unit being ordered to march via Billy-sur-Aisne and Venizel to Ste Marguerite. They reached Venizel at 9 a.m., after an hour's rest, and the Battalion then temporarily halted in column in a field by the roadside, in readiness for crossing first the railway and then the river bridge. The girders of the latter had been cut, but the reinforced concrete of the roadway was strong enough to take infantry. While waiting to pass over, enemy shellfire caused the machine-gun teams a number of casualties, heavier losses being avoided because one of the companies had just moved to shelter in a sunken road. The 11th Brigade was already across, having passed over in single file by 3 a.m. The crest was secured by a surprise attack as day was dawning; that brigade was thus the first British formation across the Aisne. The 12th Brigade was in support of the 11th and by 11.15 a.m. three of the battalions were over, including the Essex. The Brigade's advance was vividly described by Hauptmann (Captain) Bloem, who observed the movement from Chivres Ridge,as the Official History records:

Across the wide belt of meadow extending between our chain of heights and the course of the river stretched what seemed to be a dotted line formed of longish and widely separated strokes. With field glasses we could see that these strokes were advancing infantry, and unmistakably English ... From the bushes bordering the river sprang up and advanced a second line of skirmishers with at least ten paces interval from man to man. Our artillery flashed and hit – naturally, at most, a single man. And the second line held on and pushed always nearer and nearer. Two hundred yards behind it came a third wave, a fourth wave. Our artillery fired like mad; all in vain, a fifth, a sixth line came on, all with good distance and with clear intervals between the men. Splendid, we are all filled with admiration. The whole wide plain was now dotted with these funny khaki figures, always coming nearer. The attack was directed on our neighbour corps on the right (the II). And now infantry fire met the attackers, but wave after wave flooded forward and disappeared from our view behind the hanging woods that framed the entrance to the Chivres valley.

The Pompadours, after crossing, traversed the two miles of water- meadows to Bucy-le-Long in extended order, ten paces between men and 100 yards between lines, and though the shellfire was heavy, the casualties were slight. 'D' Company brought up the rear of the Essex and had an exciting time before finally joining the Battalion again. At the bridge the Company Commander could not see the remainder of the Battalion, but was advised by a sapper officer to go to the left of the road. The men crossed at the double and then broke into artillery formation just as methodically as in peacetime. At a wood close by they encountered the rear of the 2nd Lancashire Fusiliers and 'D' Company were then informed that their comrades were on the right of the road. Accordingly they inclined to the right at the double under shellfire and had arrived nearly opposite to the village of Chivres, when word came that the Battalion was at Ste

Marguerite, some hundreds of yards to the left. This intelligence was most timely, for Chivres was then held by the enemy and in such strength that later on an attack by the Lancashire Fusiliers was repulsed.

When the leading companies of the Essex reached Bucy – 12th Brigade had assembled there by 1 p.m. – word came to move to Ste Marguerite, which had been captured earlier in the day by the Rifle Brigade. After passing through the town the men climbed the wooded height to the north by means of a narrow sunken path. On arriving at the crest they occupied the open land lying to their front and also the woodland to the right, through which could be seen the beautiful Chivres Valley, with Missy in the hollow and, beyond, the thick tree-clad heights that hid Fort Condé from view. The enemy movements below could be easily observed. The Essex were ordered to cover an attack upon the Chivres trenches by the Lancashire Fusiliers. The effort was not successful owing to heavy fire from the south of Chivres village and the western slopes of the Chivres spur. The Pompadours then held the high ground north of Ste Marguerite, with their right thrown back along the eastern side of the woodland mentioned above. There they dug in and remained for the night, Lancashire Fusiliers on the right and the 1st King's Own Regiment on the left. The position was an anxious one owing to enemy activity, and for a time small-arms ammunition ran short, but this danger was relieved at 6.25 p.m. when three cartloads were received. The casualties were light, comprising ten killed and thirty-two wounded.

Writing of his experiences that day, the CO of 'B' Company tells the story of the advance:

The bridge at Venizel was found to be damaged and the King's Own and the Essex halted under cover of the village in close column of platoons and lay down. Along came a Taube [German monoplane], which dropped tinsel on us, and in five minutes shells from an 8in [210mm] battery started to arrive, causing casualties. I was soon after ordered with the men I had with me across the bridge and to advance to the high ground north of the river. This I did by sending small parties across the bridge, which when on the other side, moved in waves over the open ground under long-range shrapnel fire. When the Battalion was under the shelter of the hills it was reformed and an organised advance began towards the top of Ste Marguerite Hill. The various companies were given different jobs; mine was to clear the top of Ste Marguerite. I went up with my company in artillery formation. At the top of the hill I halted the Company and took a section forward with me to reconnoitre. We came under close-range fire from a motor gun near Vrégny village and five of the party were wounded, though not seriously. It was impossible to see far because of some entrenched positions in front, and the Company dug in behind the line of the crest, with the German artillery finding the range. About 7 p.m. we were relieved by 'A' Company and side-stepped to the east, taking a refused flank position facing Chivres. Owing to various reasons, partly the darkness of the woods, I got my line in rather a tangle, but by midnight things were fairly all right, though I did not get into touch with Battalion headquarters until next morning.

The Essex underwent a good deal of shelling and were soon busy with their spades upon a trench system. A disused cave was requisitioned as Battalion HQ and that of the support company, the only anxiety being whether there was a means of access to the enemy from the valley below. An ingenious method of lighting was adopted. Lamps were improvised by making holes in the tops of tins of rifle oil and inserting pieces of unravelled string to serve as wicks. Two Frenchmen were vastly astonished to find the Essex in possession of this cave when they came to feed the horses which they had hidden there. When the line was shortened a few days later the Battalion was able to put a company in reserve and went into real houses at Ste Marguerite, which the quartermaster made extremely comfortable. The disposition of the Battalion then was: one company in the open land to the north and another in the wood overlooking Chivres, while a third was in the cave in support and the fourth in reserve at Ste Marguerite.

'While at Ste Marguerite', wrote an officer, 'I got my first hot bath since I left England in an old wine cask sawn in half, and taken in the presence of about a dozen people.' Another wrote:

I also enjoyed a bath in that kindly wine cask, but what struck me most in the quartermaster's billet was the way the men treated the wrinkled old dame who owned the house. A typical French peasant, she had lost either her son or grandson in the war and used to sit weeping in a corner, for her sole supporter had gone and her small property was ruined. Then some Tommy employed by the quartermaster would shyly take the old gnarled hand, pat it and say, 'Tea?' The old dame understood, but she probably did not know that her cup always had besides the tea a spoonful of rum in it. The battle has since swept many times backward and forward over Ste Marguerite, and one hopes that death was merciful and spared her four years of misery.

The 11th Brigade occupied the heights from Ste Marguerite to Crouy, reinforced by 10th Brigade, and with 12th Brigade to their right. The task of 4th Division on 14 September was to move northward over the plateau between Vrégny and Crouy to aid the advance of 5th Division. But the German positions were too strongly held, for the two British divisions had against them the whole of the German II Corps as well as parts of the III and IX Corps, all from von Kluck's First Army. Meanwhile, I and II British Corps were passing the Aisne and pressing upon the Chemin des Dames, only to realise on the 15th that the limit of advance had been reached for the time being.

The deadlock was at hand. To quote the Official History: 'The 4th Division, however, as its trenches improved and as its ranks were refilled, showed much enterprise. It could do nothing on a great scale, but by pushing trenches forward and by worrying the Germans perpetually with patrols and snipers it established over them a well-marked ascendancy.' An attack by the Germans upon the British left front beyond 11th Brigade caused some loss to the Essex, whose casualties included one killed and twenty wounded. The trenches were improved during the next day, which again was full of incident, two men being killed.

The following day was comparatively quiet, only one being wounded, but the casualties were more numerous on the 17th, when one officer and seven other ranks were wounded. The eastern face of the wood was then handed over to the Lancashire Fusiliers. Between 18 and 23 September there was little to record, one man being killed and eight wounded. There was more activity on the 24th, when a patrol succeeded in getting within 150 yards of the enemy trenches and found them protected by barbed wire. At night another trench was begun, 100 yards in advance of the front line, with the intention of preparing for a forward move, and the day closed without casualty. To the end of September there was little of note, the chief episode being an early morning burst of artillery fire on the 26th. The monotony of life in the trenches was relieved by an occasional day off in the village of Ste Marguerite, where a welcome wash and rest could be secured.

October was heralded by enemy artillery fire, which, however, did no damage. At 6 p.m. the Battalion handed over the trenches to the 1st Royal Irish Fusiliers and took over a portion of the line held by 5th Division on the right. The relief was complete by 9 p.m. and the Essex marched via Ste Marguerite to Missy-sur-Aisne, taking over the defence of the village about midnight from the 1st Dorsets and the 2nd King's Own Yorkshire Light Infantry. An officer of the Essex wrote that he was fortunate enough to occupy a small house where the owner boasted a good cellar and had some bottles of a fine Macon wine. A brother officer described the post as 'an unpleasant place, as it was continually shelled. The rations came in at night and we could also hear the rumble of the German wagons. Apparently there was a tacit understanding not to interfere with each other's transport'.

It was little wonder that the spot was 'unpleasant', for the enemy were entrenched in a wood on a hill about 350 yards on the north side of the village, which entirely commanded the British positions, and sniping was frequent; 'C' Company lost a number of men from this cause. The Essex energetically improved the defences, and a route was discovered leading to a bridge of barges a quarter of a mile east of Venizel. The methodical nature of the German gunfire, which was a feature persisting throughout the campaign, was noticed on 3 October when a heavy gun threw in shells at intervals of a quarter of an hour throughout the day. The intensity of the shelling increased during the evening and work on the defences had to be stopped. The casualties were one killed and two wounded. Bombardment broke out again at ten the next morning, but this time there was response from British artillery across the Aisne, and it promptly ceased. The close of 5 October was full of incident, for the enemy briskly shelled the trenches at 5 p.m., then half an hour later they sniped the east end of the village. At 6 p.m. orders came to move on relief by French troops, only to be countermanded an hour later. On 6 October, however, came the

106

welcome news that there was to be a change of scene, and at midnight the reserve battalion of the 15th French Regiment took over. Although, at that time, it did not know its destination, the Battalion was en route for Flanders, to take part in the dreadful whirl of fighting known as the First Battle of Ypres.

XI

THE FIRST BATTLE OF YPRES
10 OCTOBER – 22 NOVEMBER

The pipedream of both the French and the British (Sir John French being much under the influence of Foch) of a breakthrough round the German right flank was now frustrated by the reconstituted German Fourth Army. So too was Falkenhayn's dream of outflanking the Allied line, although he did not yet know it. Contrary to Foch's expectations the Belgians had held firm on the line of the Yser, which made the seaward left flank temporarily secure. Thanks to King Albert's determination, his soldiers were clinging on to this last muddy corner of their country.

Ypres, a town of some size and antiquity midway between Brussels and Calais, had been famous for its textiles. It had many ancient buildings and a magnificent Cloth Hall, all later to be reduced to rubble. It was also an important road junction and, surrounded by elevations in the ground, optimistically called 'hills', was the obvious key to the whole northern front. This front, to be later known as the Salient, then extended round a sixteen-mile semi-circle, but was later to be much contracted and with a radius of five miles out from the town. Due south the British held a ten-mile long line to make contact with the French in their fifteen-mile sector, while to the north contact was made with the Belgians on the fifteen-mile line of the Yser.

The encounter battle soon developed into a soldiers' battle, those at the back crying forward and those in front crying back. It was not exactly 'back' that they cried, but 'make a stand at all costs if you can'. They could and did stand. Here was a miracle, but one aided and abetted once more by a faulty German appreciation of the situation, by the staying power of the old British regulars, and by the stopping power of their rapid small-arms fire.

The Germans made both strategic and tactical errors. By using untrained but enthusiastic levies of young men of the higher-grade student type they lost vast officer potential, mown down by the rapid fire of the British infantry and dismounted cavalry. Their experienced troops, which could have been used with far greater effect, were holding more peaceful parts of the front north of the Aisne.

There were frequent warnings to the Higher Commands of both Allies of the strength of the Germans from the sea southwards. Optimism prevailed, however, that of Sir John French alternating with the idea of a fortified camp at Boulogne when he was not under the stimulating influence of Foch. Between 10 and 18 October Foch was full of plans which, had they materialised, would have meant the complete envelopment of the Allied line. By the 20th all efforts to move forward were defeated and II Corps was actually held up by a German offensive, as were both III Corps and the Cavalry Corps. Haig's I Corps, which arrived only on 20 October, was moved to the north and also ordered to advance, but against an enemy force which had been grossly underestimated. Instead of steady advances the BEF was everywhere on the defensive and facing increasing difficulty, even in holding its ground.

British positions were therefore now established as follows: on the right II Corps west of La Bassée; then, moving northwards, III Corps and the Cavalry Corps round Messines; Rawlinson's IV Corps covering Ypres itself on the axis Menin Road-Gheluvelt; and I Corps to the north of Ypres round Langemarck. All along the front French troops were intermingled, covering gaps between formations.

Still the illusion of the possibility of an offensive continued, with orders by Foch to his own troops for an offensive towards Roulers and Thourdut. In this attack the British I Corps was asked to co-operate. Due to contradictory requests as to the direction of the British move, and to the non-appearance of the French until much later than expected, it was fortunate that the attack was defeated by the fire of the defence. If it had taken place, the BEF would once again would have had an open flank.

The German losses had been severe, and consequently they turned towards the Belgians in an attempt to break through the line of the Yser, and so capture Dunkirk and, eventually, Calais. After confused fighting the situation became so critical that, on 24 October, King Albert ordered the opening of the dykes at Nieuport so as to flood all the country between the Yser and the critical line of a railway

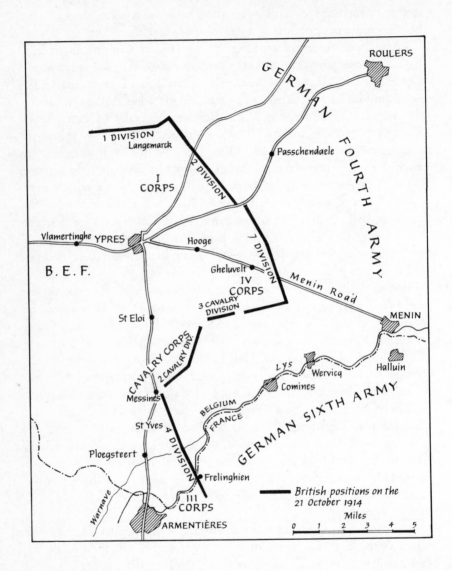

The First Battle of Ypres, 10 October–22 November 1914

embankment. The water rose slowly, but the Germans realised that if they were not to be cut off they would be obliged to retire back over the Yser, and this they did by 1 November. The seaward flank was saved.

German attacks of varying intensity had taken place all along the line from 20 October onwards, but the most severe came on the 29th with fresh troops brought from the Aisne. Met everywhere with the usual rapid fire, only cracks appeared in the line, but in an attack directed on the Messines Ridge held by the three British dismounted cavalry divisions the line was broken. The damage was repaired by the timely arrival of French reinforcements, and by German reluctance to press their attack in the face of the defenders' rapid fire.

On 31 October the main German attack, with seven fresh divisions, fell on the British 1st, 2nd and 7th Divisions. Gheluvelt on the Menin Road was a key point, since it occupied a comparatively high position and was the only place which at that time could overlook the enemy's line. Just before noon, the village was captured from the 1st Division. Two divisions, the 1st and 2nd, shared a headquarters in the Hooge Château, and Major-General S.H. Lomax, commanding 1st Division, rode back and said to Major-General Charles Monro of 2nd Division, 'My line is broken'. Shortly afterwards a shell killed or wounded almost all the occupants of the Château, including Lomax, who died of wounds later in England. For the time being control was completely lost.

Haig, who had ridden up the Menin Road with his immediate staff, 'at a slow trot as at an inspection', to see for himself the situation, was left in no doubt about its gravity. On his return to the White Château, his headquarters near 'Hellfire Corner', he received the news of the break in the line, and prepared orders for a retirement to a position covering Ypres which was to be held to the last.

News of a different kind was soon to arrive. Early in the afternoon the 1st South Wales Borderers of 1st Division, although isolated from their neighbours and reduced to a handful, had counter-attacked and retaken part of the old position on the flank. This remnant, unless reinforced, would obviously be completely unable to hold on to their small success. The 2nd Worcestershire Regiment, a meagre reserve of 2nd Division, was also positioned to aid 1st Division if the situation so warranted. It did.

Under the command of Major Hankey this battalion, also greatly under strength with only 350 men, moved up under cover for some distance. They then put in a charge which caught the Germans relaxing after their successes, and so recaptured Gheluvelt. If the situation had not been retrieved the Germans could have passed through 1st Division and outflanked the whole British position, and then have turned the French left. The way to the Channel ports would have been open. This charge by the 2nd Worcesters was one of the most brilliant feats of arms from a single battalion in the 1914-18 war, perhaps ever; in Sir John French's words 'the Worcesters saved the Empire'. Its consequences were far reaching not only in regard to the immediate tactical and strategic situation, but also for the insight it gave into the weakness of the German soldier; an inability, once having captured a position, to have enough initiative without further leadership either to consolidate or exploit it.

Both Haig and French received the news with some suspicion. French met Foch almost by chance in Vlamertinghe, due west of Ypres, and made an impassioned appeal for help for Haig's corps. Any idea of any form of withdrawal, as Haig had envisaged, was of course anathema to Foch; he had not fathomed the depths of German inertia after a success. Unless help was forthcoming, Sir John said, he would go up the line with his sentries and get himself killed, to which Foch is supposed to have replied 'You must not talk of dying, but of winning'. A promise was made for a French counter-attack on both flanks of I Corps.

A note was then drafted by Foch; the significant words in it being that 'it is essential that no retirement is made'. Under this persuasive influence French issued just such an order to Haig. The Worcesters' attack had, however, saved the situation, and only slight modifications in the line were necessary. For the next ten days Haig's line remained unchanged, except for a small withdrawal to conform with a French rearward movement on his right!

On 1 November the Messines Ridge was taken by a German night attack, but the line was held a mile further back by the arrival of the French 32nd Division and by a further French 'counter-attack' to Haig's left which, although it made no progress, had the effect of discouraging the enemy. The French took over most of the Cavalry Corps line on 2 November, and so held eighteen miles, or two thirds of the Ypres

Salient, while the central sector of the BEF's nine miles was held by the 'weary and intermixed units' of Haig's command. The 7th Division was by now reduced from 12300 to 2400 men.

Abortive local attacks were continued by the French, who by so doing played into the enemy's hands. On 6 November the Germans almost got round the rear of the British at St Eloi, and came within two miles of Ypres from the south. A promised French counter-attack did not materialise, and Haig patched up the line as best he could. On 10 November a final attack was launched against the northern hinge of the salient held by the French. This movement convinced their command that the Germans' final effort was to be against the northern sector. On the 11th the attack materialised but was less violent than might have been expected from the intensity of the bombardment. It was repulsed.

To the north of the Menin Road, however, the German 1st Guard Brigade broke through the British 1st (Guards) Brigade; a strange coincidence, although only a small remnant of a Guards battalion was left in that brigade. The Germans, bewildered once more by their success, and by the woods in which they found themselves, were attacked in the flank and driven off by the Oxfordshire and Buckinghamshire Light Infantry, in the same way as this regiment (the old 52nd Foot) had attacked the French Old Guard at Waterloo.

The failure of the 11 November attack marked the final stage of the battle, and although there were subsequent attacks, chiefly against the French, the Germans had shot their bolt. They had suffered a casualty list of 134,000 in October alone, mainly among the student volunteers; this later became known as the 'Massacre of the Innocents'.

The first Battle of Ypres was the grave of the old Regular Army; it is terrifying to think of the straits to which it was reduced in order to hold the line. Battalions landed in August over a thousand strong were on average reduced to one officer and thirty men. Cooks, officers' servants, grooms, drivers and any odds and sods capable of firing a rifle that could be mustered were at various critical moments used to patch up the rents in the line. Charges with the bayonet such as those made by the Worcesters at Gheluvelt and the London Scottish at Messines (again a sad waste of potential officers), often restored a critical situation. It was, however, the dogged defence by the old regular regiments, and the firepower produced by fifteen rounds a minute, that eventually stemmed the tide of the German mass-formation attacks.

The part played by the French and Belgians has often been underrated, or even forgotten, when mourning the loss of the old British Army. The stand made by the depleted Belgian divisions on the line of the Yser was inspired by King Albert, who wisely refused to budge from that line and who, by ordering the inundations, secured the far flank from envelopment. It was to Foch and his subordinate commanders Generals Victor d'Urbal (Eighth Army) and Pierre Dubois (IX Corps) that most was owed. Foch contributed by his refusal to counternance any form of withdrawal, and his optimism, despite the fact that it was usually based on false premises, was of great value in bolstering up the mercurial temperament of Sir John French.

The French unselfishly parted with their reserves in order to support a faltering line, and had eventually taken over the whole salient by 22 November. Neither the part they played, nor their 50,000 casualties, should be forgotten – all too easily done when grieving for the passing of the Old Army. Between the middle of October and the end of November British casualties numbered 58,000, or almost double all those before, for a total of 89,000. Battalions were often under a hundred men strong – only nine out of eighty-four exceeded three hundred.

Sir John Glubb (Glubb Pasha), in his book about his experiences as a sapper subaltern at the beginning of the 1914-18 war, wrote that in the 1960s he had read that some young intellectual (*sic*) had called the 1914 soldiers 'semi-criminal illiterates'. He went on to say: 'so fades earthly glory, turning in two generations to contemptuous sarcasm'. These soldiers may not have had university degrees, but they were simple honest men who knew their duty, and died for it. Perhaps the miscalled intellectual must always mock at everything outside his own very limited experience. The men of 1914 were not Mr Valiant – for – Truths, perhaps not even Mr Standfasts, although that is what they did. But one might hope that 'All the trumpets sounded for them on the other side'.

ONE BATTALION'S FIRST YPRES
7 OCTOBER-22 NOVEMBER

Having been relieved by the French at Missy, the Essex crossed

114

the Aisne at 2 a.m. on 7 October 1914 by the pontoon bridge at Moulin-les-Roches without interference by the enemy, and via Acy and Ecuiry came to Septmonts at 5.30 the same morning. On 8 October orders came for a move to Ambrief, the route being by Ecuiry and Chacrise. The men paraded at 9 a.m. the next day and waited till 1 p.m. Transport left for an unknown destination, but the Battalion still remained at Septmonts. It was not until 7.50 on the morning of 11 October that the Essex were taken in fifty-one motor buses to Le Meux, through Hartennes, St Remy, Villers-Cotterets, Béthancourt and Verberie.

At Le Meux the Battalion entrained and left at 9.30 p.m. by Amiens, Boulogne and Calais to Hazebrouck, which was reached at 2 p.m. on 12 October. There was some excitement in the town as a German cavalry patrol had been driven out only the day before. Early–morning gunfire was heard next day in a south-easterly direction, where the 6th Division was known to be. The enemy were in some force in the vicinity, and the Essex were soon on the move again. At 9.15 a.m. they left Hazebrouck and at 10 a.m. had reached Rouge Croix, where 6th Division on the right, and 4th Division on the left, were ordered to take the Meteren Ridge from La Couronne to Fontaine Houck, a front of five miles, while the Cavalry Corps co-operated by a movement against Berthen.

The 4th Division advance at 1.30 p.m. was upon a line from Meteren to Fontaine Houck (both inclusive), 12th Brigade having as its objective from the village of Meteren (inclusive) to a point a quarter of a mile north-east of that place. The Brigade's dispositions were Essex and 1st King's Own in the front line, with 2nd Royal Inniskilling Fusiliers and 2nd Lancashire Fusiliers in the second line, the frontage being eight hundred yards, and with a similar distance between the two lines. The dividing line between the battalions was the Rouge Croix-Les Ormes road. The 10th Brigade acted in unison on the left, the 2nd Seaforth Highlanders being next to the Essex.

The enemy, consisting of units from the 3rd and 6th Bavarian Cavalry Divisions with four *Jäger* battalions and artillery, had been located in the vicinity of the main road leading from Flêtre to Meteren. The British aim was to seize the crossroads on the Meteren side of Flêtre, to connect up with 10th Brigade, and then to advance upon Meteren itself, Essex to the left and the King's

Own taking the village. The Essex approached the position in artillery formation, two companies in the front line and two in support, and at 2.30 p.m. they reached a group of cottages on the main road near Les Ormes. The leading companies were ordered to extend on the north side of the road, but coming out from the shelter of the cottages, the men were met with heavy enfilade fire from machine guns, which were difficult to locate owing to the heavy rain and fog. The guns were believed to be posted in Meteren Church, which stood in clear outline on the hill-top. Their fire did not do much hurt, though, as the soldiers most of it whizzed harmlessly over the soldiers' heads.

The 1st Royal Warwicks, part of the advance guard (which earlier in the day had been supplied by 10th Brigade), had already reached some buildings at the foot of the hill upon which Meteren stands; they could be seen moving in the mist. The leading Essex companies came up level with them and at 3.30 p.m. a third company was also pushed forward from the support line, the fourth company later being used to prolong the line on the left. To perform this movement the fourth company had to proceed a couple of hundred yards to the left, which was accomplished by turning the men of the extended lines into file and moving across the front. 'Such a performance,' wrote an officer, 'would have driven umpires at manoeuvres frantic. We carried out the movement unscathed, however, though there was heavy machine–gun fire passing overhead. Apparently the Germans could not depress their guns sufficiently to catch us.'

The final dispositions were made under cover of some farm buildings. So sudden was the advance of the leading platoons that they leaped into the ditch forming the Meteren Becque just as the enemy became aware of the movement. Covered by their fire, the supporting platoons reached the Becque. The prospect of a successful attack did not appear promising, for three hundred yards of glacis-like slope, broken by a long hedge running diagonally across the front had to be crossed. A large farm building lay near the crest. The enemy were not visible, but the fire from the hedge was fairly heavy. The Brigade was without artillery support.

As the leading platoons climbed out of the Becque to push forward again, the Seaforth Highlanders came up on the left, prolonging the line and probably overlapping the enemy's right. The German fire slackened, and the impulse to go ahead came suddenly. The extended lines surged forward and in a few minutes the Essex were through the hedge and pushing up the hill. A few *Jägers* were captured in the farm buildings. The thick hedges of the slopes caused some confusion, and on reaching what appeared to be the top of the hill it was found to be a false crest, and it was necessary to reorganise the companies and move still farther forward. Heavy firing on the right revealed that Meteren was still occupied, and darkness was fast approaching. The Battalion bivouacked for the night on the ground it had gained, pushing forward entrenched outpost companies. Two small and apparently deserted farmhouses lay in the vicinity. Cries of 'Anglais' by the troops produced sudden movement, lights were kindled, and the buildings were found to be crowded with frightened inhabitants. Their joy was unbounded at their deliverance, and they brewed all the coffee they possessed for the good cheer of their deliverers.

The Essex had been favoured in their advance by the nature of the ground, but the King's Own, on the right, had suffered considerably. The Brigade Commander was unwilling to put his reserve, the Lancashire Fusiliers, into the fight until his right was secure, for a counter-attack was feared from that direction owing to the gap which existed between the 6th and 4th Divisions, and which was not filled until the following day. The 1st Hampshire Regiment, from divisional reserve, was accordingly placed at his disposal and in the darkness the Lancashire Fusiliers were ordered to work round the south of the village. They were stopped by gardens and wire fences, but ultimately tried the roadway from the south-west. This movement was successful and the Germans huriedly evacuated Meteren, leaving twenty-five prisoners. The place had been skilfully fortified; machine-guns placed on the roofs of houses, walls loopholed, and trenches dug outside, clear of the buildings, the whole so concealed that it was impossible to discern the defences from the front. The total casualties in the Brigade were three officers and forty-nine other ranks killed, and four officers and sixty other ranks wounded. Of these, four killed and twenty-one wounded belonged to the Essex.

Before the hours of darkness had passed, an officer of another regiment reported to the Essex that Meteren was clear of the enemy. He was very modest concerning his share in the matter, stating he had lost his way and entered the village by accident. The news was very welcome, however, and by 5 a.m. the

Battalion had pushed forward so as to look down over the plain stretching before them on the eastern side of the hill, Seaforth Highlanders being on the left of the Essex and Inniskilling Fusiliers on the right. 'As I gazed down on the plain from the top of the Meteren Hill,' wrote a combatant, 'I thought of what might have been if – well, if we had got on the hill sooner, if it had not been foggy, if the enemy had been retreating across the plain, and, lastly, if our artillery could have got up in time. I was dreaming of a gunner's paradise.'

At 9.45 the same morning, 14 October, 12th Brigade received orders to advance again, and by twelve noon was marching past Meteren. After a short rest of four hours it was on the move once more, the whole Division traversing the road to Bailleul, which the Essex reached at 8 p.m., occupying billets there for the night. One of the companies was allotted a convent in the main square. The nuns and other people gave harrowing details of the horrors perpetrated by drunken enemy soldiers on the women of the town. An Essex officer, who prided himself upon being a French scholar, was sent to find food for the officers. Approaching the nunnery, he asked the nun at the wicket gate, '*Avez vous beaucoup de faim?*' The last word he pronounced as '*femme*' and the nun, mistaking his intentions, turned very pale and rushed away from the gate, shrieking '*Les Anglais aussi!*' After a short talk, however, the nuns realised the mistake and the story was told to a delighted audience of nuns and officers that evening at dinner. They treated the Essex extremely well and the officers all got excellent beds, with the best of sheets and pillows, and, what was more, a really good wash.

At 6 p.m. the next day (15 October) 4th Division's march to Le Leuthe was resumed in an effort to secure the bridges over the Lys, a muddy stream, at Erquinghem and Pont de Nieppe west of Armentières. Two hours later a halt was called, orders being given to remain in that position until morning. The first bridge had been seized undamaged, but the Pont de Nieppe was held by machine-guns, and the Division waited until the 6th Division was across the Lys and could assist it. Part of the Battalion was lucky enough to be billeted in cottages, but the remainder had to sleep with what comfort they could upon the roadside.

By noon next day (16th) 11th Brigade was across at Erquinghem and at 4 p.m. the Pont de Nieppe was seized, a fortunate first round from an 18-pounder field-gun striking the barricade on the bridge and scaring the defenders. The 12th Brigade, on the left, occupied Ploegsteert and Hill 63, inside Belgium, guns being placed on the latter. Hill 63, over 200ft high (later to become a famous observation post), with the Château and woodland known as the Bois de Ploegsteert, on the main road from Messines to Ploegsteert, was allotted as the territory of the Essex, who reached their positions via Petit Pont with orders to extend the line eastward to Le Gheer. On 17 October 10th Brigade entered Armentières.

Early on 18 October the Essex were ordered to Ploegsteert in reserve, leaving 'C' Company at the Château as escort to the guns. At 2.50 p.m. they were on the march to Houplines on the Lys to report to GOC 10th Brigade, Brigadier-General J.A.L. Haldane, who was experiencing difficulty in seizing the difficult ground about Verlinghem. Progress remained slow in this sector. Five hours later the Essex were billeted in the southern corner of Armentières, and placed in reserve. As they were making preparations for the night's rest machine-gun and rifle fire was heard towards L'Epinette. The enemy was beginning to reveal his strength and heavy fighting was in progress, the German XIX (2nd Saxon) Corps now being in position against the British III Corps. At 6 a.m. on the 19th orders came to be ready to move after 9 a.m., the Battalion and the Inniskillings being in divisional reserve. Accordingly, at 12.30 p.m., they marched back again, via Houplines, to their original position near the Château. There the ground and billets were found to be occupied by 1st Cavalry Division, so that the Battalion went to Ploegsteert and slept once again in billets.

The 20th was a day of heavy and anxious fighting, for the enemy made some progress. Early in the morning the front of 12th Brigade, equidistant between Armentières and Pérenchies – held by the Inniskillings, the King's Own and the Lancashire Fusiliers, with the Essex in the second line trenches – was pushed hard by the enemy. The advance posts were driven in and the Germans dug in some five hundred yards from the Brigade line. The Pompadours, in support, were moved up; 'C' Company was sent to the Château at 8.30 a.m., and 'D' Company an hour later to a farm a little distance north of the River Warnave to support the King's Own and the Lancashire Fusiliers. At 4 p.m. 'A' and 'B' Companies followed 'C' Company to the Château, and they became temporarily attached to 11th Brigade for the purpose of holding Hill 63, at the north-west corner of Ploegsteert Wood, and thus securing the left flank of III Corps. 'D' Company had an anxious time near the Warnave, and at about 5.30 p.m. was also hurried up in support of 11th Brigade.

At 5.15 on the misty morning of 21 October, part of the German XIX Corps attacked the front of 12th Brigade and forced back the battalion on the left for the distance of a quarter of a mile, which enabled them to occupy Le Gheer. Not only was the safety of the Brigade seriously imperilled, but the Cavalry Corps, whose line ran northwards from St Yves to Messines, was also menaced. In these circumstances the Brigade Commander, Brigadier-General H.F.M. Wilson, ordered a counter-attack, having at his disposal for that purpose two platoons of the Essex (half 'D' Company), with two companies of the 1st East Lancashire Regiment and of the 1st Somerset Light Infantry, from 11th Brigade. The operation took place at 9 a.m., supported by the divisional artillery from Hill 63 and two squadrons (320 men, at full strength) of the 9th Lancers on the left. The Germans were severely beaten, abandoning the crossroads three-quarters of a mile north of Le Touquet, on the Lys opposite Frélinghien, and suffering heavy casualties. There were 134 prisoners, while 45 men of the Inniskillings were released. The crossroads were safely held by the East Lancashires for the rest of the day against all enemy movements. The 12th Brigade's losses had been considerable, however, numbering 468 officers and men, of which 184 were from the King's Own.

The operation at Le Gheer, in which Nos 13 and 15 Platoons of 'D' Company were concerned, was a praiseworthy affair, and it reflected considerable credit on the Pompadours. It will be remembered that the Company had been sent to reinforce the line about a couple of miles south-east of the village of Le Gheer. There, it was decided to retain only two platoons, which were left in support of another part of the line, while the Company Commander, with the other two platoons, reported to Brigade HQ in Ploegsteert. There he received orders to move to a road junction just north of Le Gheer to support the 9th Lancers. On arrival the men, tired out, for they had had no rest for several days, slept in some empty houses and at dawn dug themselves in along the edge of Ploegsteert Wood, where there was a small ditch.

At 6 a.m. on 21 October came information that the enemy appeared to be in possession of Le Gheer. There was no time for reconnaissance, and the platoons were doubled diagonally through the wood with the object of getting between Le Gheer and Ploegsteert, and then working forward until they came out on the main road. No. 13 Platoon went through the wood to occupy a position facing Le Gheer. Complete surprise was achieved, for, breaking out suddenly, they caught the enemy with enfilade fire as they lay by the roadside, waiting for the situation to develop, and effectively stayed the advance in that quarter for the time being. The 'D' Company platoons were not forced to retire, for the Brigade staff captain, who had been sent forward to act as guide to two companies of the East Lancashires, came up, bringing 15 and 16 Platoons forward. Though both platoons suffered loss from enfilade machine-gun fire, they took part in the charge which recovered Le Gheer, No. 15 being with the 9th Lancers and No. 13 with the East Lancashires. The wood was cleared, the village occupied and the forward trench taken. The enemy charged No. 13 Platoon three times, but were driven off.

Nos 14 and 16 Platoons also saw hard fighting on the 21st, being in support on the left flank of the King's Own, to the east of Le Gheer. It was savage and successful fighting, though not without severe casualties, for of 'D' Company one officer was killed, one wounded and one taken prisoner, and sixty-six other ranks were also killed, wounded and missing.

The stirring events of 21 October 1914 were not to end the participation of the Essex in the First Battle of Ypres. The next day the Battalion, having taken over from the 5th Dragoon Guards, was at Messines, and repulsed an enemy attack in the early morning; that, however, had little heart in it. At 8 p.m. the same day another effort was made against them by means of mobile machine-guns, the latter being fixed upon motor-cars, but again the attempt was easily beaten off.

About this time 'B' Company had an exciting experience when in divisional reserve. Orders were issued to rendezvous at Despierre Farm for a counter-attack, in which it would be employed with two companies of the King's Own and one of the Rifle Brigade. At the farm the three other companies were hurried off elsewhere and 'B' Company was left on its own. Orders were not to get engaged unless it was absolutely necessary, but, after consultation with the staff captain of 12th Brigade, it was decided to carry out the operation. The whole company was put into one line and the bluff attack succeeded, principally because a relief of German troops was proceeding at the time, so that the Essex were not spotted until within thirty yards of the trenches. The enemy hastily evacuated the trenches at Despierre Farm crossroads, which, filled with the dead of both nations, were reoccupied, a half-hearted counter-attack being beaten off. In a small house at the corner were found three men, an officer, company sergeant-major and signaller, all dead, but with no marks on them. The house had been heavily shelled during the day.

On the 23rd, at 5.30 a.m., the trenches were handed over to the 1st Connaught Rangers, from 2nd Division, and the Essex were marched to the north-west of Messines in support of 1st Cavalry Division. Before long another move was made and at 4.30 p.m. they left to rejoin 12th Brigade at Le Bizet, the headquarters marching via Wulverghem. On arrival in the early evening supplies were issued by the roadside, but there was little respite and at 7 p.m. the Battalion, with the rest of the Brigade, relieved 17th Brigade of 6th Division as far as the Rue du Bois, the 4th Division having a front of over eight miles. To add to the discomfort of an unpleasant position, the Essex were attacked as soon as they were established in the trenches, though happily without effect. For the next two days sniping and shelling caused several casualties, which made even more welcome the arrival of a reinforcement draft of nearly a hundred men.

The weather had turned wet and cold and the night of 26 October was very uncomfortable, for the trenches were full of water and mud and, to add to the discomfort, there was some shelling by high explosive. Relieved by the Inniskillings the same evening, the Battalion went into reserve in Armentières. The Corps Commander, General Pulteney, had issued instructions for the trenches to be deepened and improved, and went on to say that divisional commanders should withdraw as many men as possible from the front line to the support line, and thus relieve the front line frequently. They were also to collect a strong divisional reserve outside German artillery range, and so obtain thorough rest for the men.

The 4th Division achieved considerable repute for its steadiness during these critical days, and the official historians of the war wrote of it:

The Division was left with the impression that by straight shooting over the parapet, backed up by crossfire of artillery and flanking fire of machine-guns, it could stop a German attack of almost any weight. The action of the divisional artillery was extraordinarily effective and arrangements were made by which it was possible to switch nearly the whole of it on to any sector that was menaced, except that near Le Gheer, where the high trees of Ploegsteert Wood gave protection to the enemy. The guns were kept under divisional control, but the infantry brigades had a call on particular batteries in case of need.

Long rest for the Essex was not to be had, for at 6 a.m. on 27 October the order came to stand to, there being heavy artillery fire. In the afternoon 'A' and 'B' Companies moved to the crossroads at La Chapelle d'Armentières; the former for outpost duty and in the second line of trenches, with 'B' in support, the latter also providing a working party. There was much tension during the night owing to enemy activity, and then at 6 p.m. on the 28th the Pompadours relieved the Inniskillings in the trenches about a thousand yards south of the Pont Egal railway crossing.

Although German snipers were active all day on the 29th, little damage was done, the casualties comprising one killed and two wounded. The Battalion should have been relieved by the Inniskillings the next day, but the latter had to be hurried to the support of 11th Brigade. In the early morning of 31 October the enemy attacked, but the movement had no heart in it and was repulsed without loss.

The closing days of the First Battle of Ypres constituted a period of great anxiety to III Corps, on account of the extended front, absence of reserves and the exhaustion of the troops. They also brought very heavy shelling for the Essex, who suffered several casualties. On 1 November the snipers were very active and there was gunfire on the forward trenches. One shell pitched into a party of 'A' Company, killing three and wounding one, while two others were killed and two wounded, but on the 3rd the artillery was quiet, although the same number of casualties was suffered. The 4th was a day of much enemy effort. In the morning, during a thick fog, the Germans tried to break into the line held by 'D' Company beside the railway, but they were repulsed with ease. Then 'A' Company's trenches received attention, being considerably damaged by shellfire, though without serious injury to the garrison.

At 7.40 p.m. on 4 November came welcome relief by the 2nd Leinster Regiment, and the Essex went into billets at La Chapelle d'Armentières. A day's rest, and on the evening of the 6th the King's Own handed over their line, running from the Lille-Chapelle d'Armentières road to a point four hundred yards north of Rue du Bois. Casualties were slight during this tour of duty, but the Germans were active and constant firing was heard in the direction of Ploegsteert and Messines. So 11 November, the fateful day upon which the famous attack by the Prussian Guard was repulsed near Ypres, closed in this sector with considerable fighting. The night was dark, the wind blowing at hurricane strength and the rain constantly pouring down. During the height of the storm the Germans attacked the Rue du Bois, accompanied by much shelling, which set several farms alight, the wildness of the night thus being lit by blazing homesteads. There was an enemy effort on the left of the Battalion, but it was repulsed at a cost of two killed and twelve wounded, though machine-guns and rifles jammed owing to the mud and rain.

Shrapnel and high-explosive were rained upon the Essex at 3 p.m. on each of the next two days, and then came relief by the Leinsters. Yet it was a change of scene and not rest that was intended, for by the evening of the same day, the 14th, the Battalion was in trencnes formerly occupied by the Hampshires, running from Le Gheer crossroads to the River Warnave – ground with which it was already familiar. Shelling caused eleven casualties (three killed) on the 16th and 17th, and on the 18th 'A' Company, in reserve at the edge of Ploegsteert Wood, suffered several casualties, losing six men killed and fourteen wounded. On the same day (20th) that the East Lancashires relieved the Essex, the latter took over from the Inniskillings on a line from Warnave level-crossing to the neighbourhood of Le Touquet. The trenches in this sector were in poor condition, with practically no communication ways. Six casualties marked the last day of the First Battle of Ypres.

On 22 November a company of the 2nd Monmouthshire Regiment was attached for instructional purposes. The day was remembered because four platoons, or one company, were sent to Nieppe for bathing, and this much-appreciated innovation was described by one private as 'just like a birthday after being up to the neck in mud and water'. The whole Battalion was sent in parties of four platoons to Nieppe and its gigantic wash was completed by the 29th, a day which the Germans celebrated by firing forty-one shells at a working party and doing no damage.

XII

THE ROYAL FLYING CORPS

It is not by oversight that the work of the infant Royal Flying Corps has yet to be mentioned. On the contrary, its importance, and the fledgling use of powered road transport in the early stages of the war, are of sufficient interest for each to merit a separate chapter.

The horse has had an almost hypnotic influence on the military mind. Besides saying 'Ha! Ha!' among the Biblical trumpets, this ubiquitous animal was rated by the poet Rudyard Kipling second only to 'women' as being 'greater than all things are', and even superior to 'power' and 'war'. The tradition has endured.

Many years after World War I, senior officers in infantry battalions were still mounted, and in 1936 much of the transport used by the German Army in manoeuvres on the Belgian frontier was horsed, as it would be throughout World War II. Even in 1940 a whole British cavalry division, in the strictest sense of that term, was stationed in Palestine. Pre-1914 squabbles about the future role of cavalry have already been mentioned, but the truth of the matter was that this animal, more fortunate than man as regards future wars, became obsolete to cavalrymen on the Messines Ridge. General Sir Edmund Allenby's campaign in Palestine in 1917-18 was of course a brilliant exception; at Kifri in Iraq in 1943 there were still entrenchments from which the Turks had faced probably the last cavalry charge by British forces, late in 1918. Since it was made uphill it must have finished much as did the French cuirassiers against the squares at Waterloo, but by then the Turks had had enough.

The popular belief that all-1914 generals were cavalrymen (and therefore stupid) is nonsense, but indifference rather than opposition was largely the attitude of military officialdom to mechanisation in any form. Lord Roberts, one old soldier ever interested in what was new, wrote to Field-Marshal Sir William Nicholson, the Chief of the

Imperial General Staff, some years before the war to ask what was being done about military aviation. The reply is illuminating: 'As regards aeroplanes we maintain an open mind and hope not to be behind, but so far I am not quite convinced about their military value. To sustain themselves in the air they necessarily have to move at a very high speed. As regards dropping explosives with any attempt at accuracy there is nothing to guide us in forming an opinion. Dirigible airships are of course in a different category and may perhaps be more formidable than aeroplanes!' It is only surprising that he did not call them 'flying machines'.

For the French, Foch, both terse and damning, simply said in 1910 'That is good sport but for the Army the aeroplane is useless'. To anticipate, it may be said that air reconnaissance observed the German attempt to outflank the BEF at Mons, and of greater value still was its spotting of von Kluck's inward turn before Paris which comprised the original Schlieffen Plan. No bad record for something of 'no military value'.

On 17 December 1903 the Wright brothers made the first powered flights in the teeth of a gusty wind at a speed of thirty-five miles per hour; one flight being at an altitude of not more than ten feet. During 1904, after an unfortunate start, more than a hundred flights were made, with considerable success. Few people, however, really believed in the Wrights' invention. The US Government was not interested, and between 1906 and 1908 it was three times refused by the British Government, twice by the War Office and once by the Admiralty. After considerable developments in Germany with the Zeppelin from 1900, and in France with various 'flying machines' and aero engines, flying was much publicised through the crossing of the English Channel by Louis Blériot on 25 July 1909. Britain was left well behind.

Since this book is about the early battles of 1914 it would be tedious to go into too much detail about the early struggles of a few dedicated officers, largely at their own expense, to become pilots, and eventually to create the Royal Flying Corps on 13 May 1912.

The RFC took the field at the outbreak of war under the command of Brigadier-General Sir David Henderson, KCB, DSO, with Lieutenant-Colonel F.H. Sykes as his General Staff Officer I, Major H. R. Brooke-Popham as Deputy Assistant Quartermaster–General, Captain W. G. H. Salmond as GSO II, and Lieutenant B. H. Barrington

Kennett as Deputy Assistant Adjutant-General and Quartermaster-General. The force consisted of this headquarters 2, 3, 4 and 5 Squadrons, and an aircraft park.

Each squadron of twelve aircraft was to mobilise at its normal peacetime station, ready to move on the fourth day. The forty-eight aeroplanes (out of the RFC's 179 machines of all types) were to move by air first to Dover, and thence, on the sixth day, to the appointed field in the theatre of war. The horses (*sic*), horse vehicles and motor-bicycles, with the baggage and supplies, were to travel by road to the port of embarkation, and from there be shipped to the overseas base.

It is interesting to note the articles that were to be carried by the pilots flying to France. Besides revolvers, field glasses, a spare pair of goggles and a roll of tools, they were ordered also to carry a water bottle containing boiled water, a small stove and, in the haversack, biscuits, cold meat, a piece of chocolate and a packet of 'soup-making material'.

Headquarters left Farnborough on the 11th and reached Amiens on 13 August. The aircraft park left Avonmouth on the 17th and arrived at Boulogne on the night of the 18th, there to be greeted by the landing officer with deep suspicion. He forthwith dispatched a wire to GHQ: 'An unnumbered unit without aeroplanes which calls itself an aircraft park has arrived. What are we to do with it?' It did, however, eventually move to Amiens to make an advanced base for the squadrons already at Maubeuge.

The squadrons flew to France. The details of their somewhat adventurous flights need not be recorded here, except to say that they were indeed eventful with numerous accidents, none fortunately fatal. One unlucky member of No. 5 Squadron made a forced landing near Boulogne and was imprisoned by the French for nearly a week!

It should perhaps be mentioned here that No. 1 Squadron had been originally a dirigible airship squadron, and was in the process of changing over to aeroplanes; it was not to go to France until later. Before the war there had been much controversy about the best type of aeroplane for general use: all, of course, had their limitations, but naturally one type of machine for one squadron was an ideal. At this time as there was no formation-flying; each machine was on its own and uniformity was of less importance. Nos 2 and 4 Squadrons had BE2 machines throughout, No. 3 had Blériots and Henri Farmans, and

No. 5 Henri Farmans, Avros and BE8s. All the engines were French: France herself mustered 136 aircraft against Germany's 180.

Like the rest of the BEF, the RFC was received with great enthusiasm, bar the unfortunate in prison, the usual shower of flowers, fruit, wine and kisses being bestowed upon them. The hardships of war were yet to come, but there were already casualties. An officer and his mechanic were killed on the 16th in a crash on the aerodrome at Amiens, and on the 18th an officer broke several bones and his corporal mechanic was killed when they crashed at Péronne; both machines were BE8s.

On 16 August, HQ and Nos 2, 3 and 4 Squadrons moved from Amiens to Maubeuge. The RFC was now in the war zone, but still all was peace. The British Army had not yet appeared, but one evening British troops marched through Maubeuge on their way to Mons. 'We were rather sorry they had come', said Captain Philip Joubert de la Ferté later, 'because up to that moment we had only been fired on by the French whenever we flew. Now we were fired on by French and English ... To this day I can remember the roar of musketry that greeted two of our machines as they left the aerodromes and crossed the main Maubeuge-Mons road along which a British column was proceeding.' To guard against incidents like this the RFC, by working all night, painted a union flag on the underside of the lower planes of all the machines. This sign was often difficult to distinguish, however, and was later replaced by the roundel that has remained to this day.

The first reconnaissances were carried out by the RFC on 19 August. The pilots were the twenty-six year-old Captain Joubert de la Ferté of No. 3 Squadron in a Blériot, and Lieutenant G.W. Mapplebeck of No. 4 Squadron in a BE2. They started at 9.30 a.m. and flew without observers. Captain Joubert was to reconnoitre the Nivelles-Genappe area to report on what Belgian forces were in that neighbourhood, and Mapplebeck was to find out whether enemy cavalry were still in force in the neighbourhood of Gembloux. The machines were to fly together as far as Nivelles 'so that if one was obliged to descend the other could report its whereabouts', but they lost their way and lost each other. Mapplebeck eventually found himself over a large town, which he failed to recognise as Brussels.

Joubert, in a slower machine, attempted to steer by compass through bands of cloud and after two hours of wandering landed at Tournai.

He made inquiries concerning the Belgian Army but nothing was known of it. He left Tournai at 12.15 p.m., lost his way again, and at 2 p.m. landed at Courtrai. Here he was told by the *gendarmerie* that the headquarters of the Belgian Flying Corps was at Louvain. He left Courtrai at 3 p.m., and passed over Ath, Hal, Braine l'Alleud, and Nivelles, and returned to Maubeuge at 5.30 p.m. He reported occasional trains in the main stations and pickets on the road to Brussels.

Between the 20th and 22nd eighteen reconnaissances were carried out, eventually revealing large bodies of troops approaching the British front. Most of these reconnaissances met with rifle fire and Sergeant-Major Jittings was wounded in the leg, the first soldier to be wounded in an aeroplane. The most important report stated that a long column, whose strength was estimated as that of an army corps, had been observed; this was in fact von Kluck's II Corps, and the reports seemed to show an attempt at an enveloping movement. The same report confirmed what had already been seen, the presence of enemy troops moving on Soignies along the great *chaussée*.

On this day, the 22nd, a machine failed to return from over enemy territory – it was bringing down this machine that gave the Germans the first evidence of the BEF's presence. (The observer's report, so far as he had written it, was picked up near the wreckage of the machine by some Belgian peasants, and eventually found its way to the War Office.) Air reports on the 22nd had given some indication of the success of von Bülow's Second Army in crossing the Sambre, and had further shown a possible enveloping movement in the direction of Gramont, as well as giving an indication of German strength opposed to the BEF.

On the following day, the 23rd, the RFC kept up continuous flights over and behind the battlefield of Mons, giving information not only of German movements but also, more important still, of the position of their artillery. The retreat began on the 24th and the continued movement to the rear put considerable strain on RFC HQ, which was also obliged to move almost daily to select new aerodromes or landing grounds. Between 16 August and 4 September no fewer than ten changes of location had to be made, each bringing attendant complications, mostly concerned with transport. While the aerodromes were changing almost daily the pilots carried out reconnaissances, often starting out not knowing in whose hands their aerodrome might be on their return.

On the 24th, an observation of the German advance at about 4 a.m. showed what proved to be part of von Kluck's II Corps on a line of march that would take it to the west of the BEF's extreme western flank. This line of advance, well to the west of the British line of retreat, was held on the following morning, for von Kluck believed that the next BEF position after Mons would be on a line having its right resting on the fortress of Maubeuge. The troops observed by these two reconnaissances were meant to envelop the British but, as has already been seen, the lure of Maubeuge was resisted by Sir John French, and this German movement closed on air.

During the Battle of Le Cateau much valuable information was given by pilots to Sir Horace Smith-Dorrien regarding the stability of his front. This was subsequently relayed to GHQ, although how it was received there by French and Murray is a matter for considerable speculation.

On the evening of 30 August von Kluck received the famous message from Second Army HQ reporting a decisive victory and asking First Army to wheel inwards towards the line La Fère-Laon. Von Kluck replied that First Army had wheeled round towards the Oise and on the 31st would advance by Compiègne and Noyon to exploit the success of Second Army. This was the wheel which upset the Schlieffen Plan, and was discovered by the British from the air. It must be emphasised that this movement by von Kluck, although instigated by von Bülow, was confirmed as being in order by the German Supreme Command, presumably to implement the Kaiser's wishes regarding the 'contemptible little army'. No fewer than three reports by British pilots all confirmed the truth of this inwards turn.

It would be impossible in one chapter to detail further the magnificent work of the pilots and observers. It is enough to say that all von Kluck's principal moves were spotted and reported to GHQ, so Sir John French was well served by his new arm. At first air reports were regarded with some suspicion, but their value in helping the British Army escape from the German trap was swiftly realised. Many difficulties apart from flying were encountered, from enemy cavalry patrols to actual ground encounters due to the rapidly changing situation. On 31 August, while the RFC occupied Senlis racecourse, two officers motored to Paris to get some aircraft spares, and returned in the evening to find the Germans in occupation. They were mistaken for German officers and drove their car right up to the cottages which a few hours earlier had been theirs – somehow they managed to escape.

During the Battle of the Marne there came about an important development, which was the detachment of squadrons to report direct to the two British corps commanders, and in each squadron there was an additional radio aeroplane to provide wireless communication with RFC HQ. By November, wings had been created to support each corps, and later wings were combined to form brigades in support of each army. Reconnaissance work naturally continued during the Battle of the Aisne and after the BEF move north. The corresponding German denuding of their Aisne trenches, also to move troops north, was spotted, but unfortunately their later, massive, movement against the Ypres line went undetected.

During the early days of the Battle of First Ypres no important information could be obtained about German strategic or immediate tactical movements due to bad weather. The main RFC task was to plot railheads, camps and dumps, but of far greater importance was the spotting of German batteries, thus avoiding a waste of precious artillery ammunition. The shortage of the latter was now beginning to be felt (by the end of October the BEF's guns were rationed to nine rounds each per day), and was later to become a major military-political crisis. Aerial photography, still in its infancy, was improving daily, as was the development of radio, still chiefly the province of only one squadron. The Italians had carried out the very first aircraft bombing in their 1911-12 war with Turkey, but during the retreat the dropping of bombs remained highly experimental; there was no bomb-dropping gear but hand-grenades were stuffed into pockets, and large bombs carried on the person.

The retreat also witnessed the beginnings of air combat. No. 5 Squadron had made early experiments with machine-guns, but there was no special armament. Officers carried revolvers and sometimes carbines; and on one occasion a German plane was destroyed by skilful manoeuvre which forced it to the ground. One incident that occurred just after the First Battle of Ypres must conclude this brief account of the RFC's work. It is taken direct from the first volume of *The War in the Air*, and 'it serves to illustrate how the air work of the Germans may sometimes have been impeded by a certain defect of sympathy in the German officer class':

German two-seater machines were commonly piloted by non-commissioned officers, who took their orders from the officer in the observer's seat. On 22 November Lieutenants L. A. Strange and F. G. Small of No. 5 Squadron were returning from a reconnaissance, flying a height of about seven thousand feet. The machine, an Avro with an 80-hp Gnôme engine, carried a Lewis gun, which had been mounted by them, against orders, on rope tackle of their own devising, just above the observer's seat. In the air they met a new German Albatross with a 100-hp Mercedes engine. They showed fight at once. Diving from a height of five hundred feet above the German machine and at right angles to its line of flight, they turned underneath it and flew along with it, a little in front and less then a hundred feet below. From this position, which they maintained while both machines made two complete turns in the air, they were able to empty two drums of ammunition into the German machine. After the second drum the pilot lost his nerve, and the machine side slipped away and down, landing behind our lines close to Neuve-Eglise. There were twenty bullet holes in the German machine but the pilot and observer were both uninjured. The British officers landed close by to claim their prisoners. The German observer, a commissioned officer, took little notice of them. As soon as his machine landed he jumped out of it and, dragging the partner of his dangers and triumphs out of the pilot's seat, knocked him down, and began to kick him heavily about the body. If ever a collection of incidents shall be made, under the title 'How the War was Lost and Won', to illustrate the causes of things, this little drama will deserve a place in it.

Unfortunately, it did not need a sense of humour for German pilots to direct shellfire on the Hooge Château.

XIII

MOTORISATION

The brave Lord Mayor in coach and pair,
King Edward, in his motor.
'The Ballad of Hampstead Heath', *James Elroy Flecker*

When Flecker wrote these lines he was using the word 'brave' to mean triumphant, colourful, perhaps a bit showy, rather than courageous. This explanation is entirely superfluous to the story to follow, although it does demonstrate that words do have a way of changing their meanings in a remarkably short space of time. The next line is the important one. The motor-car had become a going concern by the end of the century and was taken up by those who could afford, it often in imitation of their sovereign. Unfortunately the Army, or rather the War Office, remained apathetic to the lead given by their titular head.

The French, the pioneers of the motor-car with such as firms as Panhard and de Dion, were not so prejudiced, and early in the twentieth century saw the possibilities of the internal combustion engine as the motive power for the rapid transport of the machine-gun.

As will be seen later, both the taxi-cab and the London omnibus were to have considerable parts to play as means of improvised transport. As early as 1905 a naval officer suggested that taxi-cabs might be used by sailors landed from a warship in aid of the civil power. They were to carry a driver and one sailor as a gunner, though how many taxis, each manned by one sailor, were considered necessary to quell a good-sized riot, or could be carried by a warship, did not come up for consideration by the Lords of the Admiralty. The original proposal, although well meant, was in its embryo stage considered impractical.

At the beginning of the war there was practically no motor transport in regular use by the British Army, yet the mobilised BEF possessed 1200 transport lorries as against a mere 500 for five of the seven German armies in the West. Commercial vehicles were requisitioned still in their original paint, and motor-buses, again in their familiar red coats, went to Antwerp and later, in less familiar khaki, were used in larger numbers when the BEF was transferred to the Ypres area. All the continental armies found themselves short of motorised transport in 1914, although subsidies had been paid to private owners to buy vehicles that could be easily converted on the outbreak of war. The fascination with taxis and buses was, however, fully justified, as is proved by the 'taxis of the Marne' and the various uses put to buses by both the British and French armies. Early in October Sir John French asked for 300 buses to carry his infantry, and by that month's end there were four Army bus companies in existence.

There were, however, to be far more important developments than the improvisations, which even included staff cars driven by their enthusiastic private owners, who thus saw, if not the battle, at least the comings and goings of both the great and not-so-great. When the war broke out the Naval Wing of the Royal Flying Corps had already been separated from the Military Wing, and had become the Royal Naval Air Service or RNAS. It is not, however, their flying duties, more varied than those of the RFC, which can be recounted here. On 25 August 1914 Wing Commander Samson (Commander, RN) was ordered to take his squadron to Ostend, where they were to co-operate with a force of Royal Marines. Samson had already been a pioneer – in June 1912, when flying the first Short seaplane, he had transmitted radio signals up to ten miles.

The whole force arrived safely. Samson himself was fired at by rifles as he was coming down, and after landing was stalked by a couple of Royal Marines 'who had come to Belgium to shoot Germans and were aching to get to work'. The force remained at Ostend for three days only. There was no artillery and the Marine Brigade had only about half-a-dozen machine-guns, the defence of Ostend against a German attack in force would have been more than difficult.

On the suggestion of General Aston, who commanded this Marine Brigade, Wing Commander Samson made a motor-car reconnaissance as far as Thournout and Bruges in two cars, one of them fitted with a maxim gun.

At Bruges [wrote Samson] we were received with great enthusiasm, the streets being crowded with people. The popular delusion which we did not contradict, was that we were the advance party of a large British army. The Civil Guard hastily donned their uniform on our arrival and turned out briskly with weapons and valour. They used, we found out later, to be quick-change artists, from uniform to plain clothes and vice versa, according to circumstances. Having gained some information in the town we returned to Ostend. The whole party enjoyed themselves immensely, although some of the more bloodthirsty members were disappointed at not getting a fight. *This trip made us consider the question of motor-car operations and ideas were discussed for armouring the cars.* [Author's italics.]

The force, ordered back to England, gained a reprieve but was directed by the Admiralty to operate from Dunkirk: 'The Admiralty desires to reinforce officer commanding aeroplanes with fifty to sixty armed motor-cars and two to three hundred men. This small force will operate in conformity with the wishes of the French military authorities but we hope it may be accorded a free initiative.'

This little naval force began at once to operate from Dunkirk carrying out reconnaissance by aeroplane and using motor-cars for raids on the flank of the German communications. It gave assistance to the French and put heart into the much-tried civil population of Belgium. Most of the work at first was done with motor-cars for the aeroplanes were few in number.

It would not be possible to give in detail here all the exploits of Wing Commander Samson. For one short period even Lille was occupied, and for good measure, he issued a note to the authorities to that effect, signing it 'Officer in Command of English Force at Dunkirk'. This was done to try to impress upon the Germans that there was a large number of British troops about the place. A fight at Cassel, where the Germans suffered considerable casualties, much impressed not only the local inhabitants but also the home authorities. The motor-car work was daily gaining in importance; what was needed was a stronger force and armoured cars. The First Lord of the Admiralty (Winston Churchill) and the Director of the Air Department (Captain Murray Sueter, RN) were ready and willing to support this enterprise. On 8 September 250 Marine reservists arrived in Dunkirk, and detailed plans were worked out for future operations.

Aeroplanes, and also the local *gendarmerie,* daily watched the movement of German troops along the roads, and motor-cars, sometimes assisted by the infantry, carried out sweeps to surround parties of German horsemen or cyclists. There were several fights. On 13 September there was a brush with some German cavalry patrols just outside the town of Doullens. Three horsemen were killed and one was severely wounded. The wounded man died later, and was found to be carrying a child's atlas with which to find his way about the country. The map of France was about three inches square, with only the names of a few towns on it.

It was now necessary to find an advanced inland base and the village of Morbecque, about three miles south of Hazebrouck, was chosen. Two aeroplanes and six armoured cars and lorries were the equipment for the headquarters, together with 187 marines and 31 naval ratings. Most of the work continued to be done by the motor-cars. Some of the lorries were armoured by a shipbuilding firm at Dunkirk, and new armoured cars began to arrive from England. A cyclist force was organised from the Marines, and a number of French boys who knew the country well were formed into a Boy Scout unit.

The main idea of these preparations was to organise more important attacks on the German lines of communication between Lille and Valenciennes. The troops for this purpose were to consist of a brigade of French territorials, a squadron of Algerian cavalry known (here and in the Italian campaign of World War II) as 'goumiers', and a battery of '75s'. The RNAS was to operate with as big a force of armoured cars as possible under the French general in command.

On 22 September the French troops occupied Douai. The cars had several sharp engagements on the roads round that town, but German pressure was growing, making any form of harassing or reconnaissance action difficult. What were to have been attacks on the German lines of communication now became the defence of Douai.

In extricating the French from the besieged town the armoured cars played a significant and dangerous part, clearing the way for a considerable number of the garrison to get out of the town in safety. Commander Samson's action was highly commended by both French and English generals; the report to the Admiralty saying that 'Commander Samson and all ranks appear to have behaved very gallantly in difficult circumstances'.

The fall of Antwerp, recorded elsewhere, put paid to the adventures of Commander Samson and his force. What might have been accomplished with a large number of both men and armoured vehicles, using aircraft for eyes, is of course mere speculation. Could it have been possible that someone with imagination, in view of the static warfare now developing, might have foreseen the tank as the logical outcome of such operations?

Samson was a real *Boys' Own Paper* type of swashbuckler, a much-needed bit of colour at a particularly sombre moment in time. But he was not the only colourful figure. Another, although of a very different hue, was Hugh Richard Arthur Grosvenor, Second Duke of Westminster, known to his friends as Bend Or from the blazoning of the family coat-of-arms. He was probably at that time the richest man in Britain, owning as he did, among much else, a large part of Mayfair.

The Duke of Westminster was not entirely without military experience. He had served for a short time in the Blues (Royal Horse Guards), and had been an ADC to Lord Roberts during the South African War. On the outbreak of war in 1914 he was offered a job at home by Kitchener, which he turned down. He had then transported himself, his blue and silver Rolls-Royce, and his personal chauffeur to France, where he attached himself to Sir John French with a roving commission.

It is said that one of the reasons why he welcomed the war was that it saved him from fighting a duel against a French nobleman with whose wife he had had an affair. While driving staff officers, or while looking for trouble, he had also witnessed the gallant but costly charge of the 9th Lancers at Quiévrain behind Mons on 24 August, and had rescued Captain Francis Grenfell, who had been wounded while leading his squadron, and who won the VC for helping save 119th Battery's six 18-pounders. It was said that the Duke should have had a decoration, but since he had no official capacity, and was *persona non grata* with Kitchener, there could be no possibility of any tangible distinction.

At the beginning of the war, the Royal Automobile Club was asked by the War Office to recruit a number of drivers to go to France in order to make generals and staff officers more mobile, once again showing how the possibilities of motor transport had been neglected.

Among those thus employed were two men who had resigned their commissions and were considered too old to fight. One, C. D. Baker-Carr, was later reinstated in the army and rose to the rank of brigadier-general. The other was Toby Rawlinson, brother of Sir Henry, the eventual commander of IV Corps. Toby had served in the 17th Lancers but had become famous as a racing-driver, and a manufacturer of racing cars in Paris. He also had an enclyopaedic knowledge of the roads in the north of France and Belgium. With these assets and a car capable of 80 mph he became the acknowledged leader of the 'civilian' chauffeurs.

The career of these drivers only lasted a few months, but without them the BEF's communications would have been seriously affected. Many went armed; Rawlinson himself bought two machine-guns from a gunsmiths in Cannon Street, thus laying himself open to being shot as a *franc-tireur* had he been captured by the Germans.

In his book *Chauffeur to Brigadier-General*, Baker-Carr tells an amusing story of how, on one of the numerous GHQ moves to the rear, Uhlans were reported to be roving the countryside, which, true or false, was a pretty normal occurrence. On their way a car was seen coming at high speed in the opposite direction. When it stopped it was found to be Bend Or's Rolls, the chauffeur then explaining that His Grace had left his cigar case in the billet he had occupied the night before! However, long journeys with vital messages or the transportation of staff officers were the order of the day, and much excitement was had by all. C.D. Baker-Carr also wrote that, when driving generals and staff officers around after the Battle of Le Cateau, during the Retreat from Mons, they often encountered small parties of men. The following dialogue inevitably took place: 'Who are you?' 'We are the sole survivors of the Blankshire Regiment; all the rest got done in yesterday: not a soul except us is alive.' 'All right, keep straight on for a couple of miles and you will find three or four hundred other sole survivors of your regiment.' This said Baker-Carr, happened at least twenty times.

The Duke of Westminster returned to England after the fall of Antwerp to order things in a more regular way. He came back to France as a lieutenant-commander, RNVR, with a fleet of armoured cars provided at his own expense. These cars or their counterparts saw service chiefly in the Middle East against the Senussi, and in Iraq up to World War II.

Toby Rawlinson, illegally gazetted a colonel by Sir John French, became, after organising a mobile anti-aircraft defence in London, an almost legendary figure in the Near East quite in the tradition of John Buchan's Sandy Arburthnot, both at the end of the war and later, when the situation in Turkey became critical. His was a type now probably extinct,chiefly through lack of opportunities.

XIV

TO FIGHT ANOTHER DAY 1914/1940

Retreat is an ugly word, and not popular in the military vocabulary. Popularity, however, is ever fickle, and facts have to be faced; it is absurd to say that such a word is unknown in some greater or lesser formations of an army. Sir John Moore's retreat to Corunna in 1808-9, a classic example in British military history, was closely followed during Wellington's campaigns in the Iberian Pensinula, by other retreats conducted with masterly skill. In the two retreats under consideration here, Mons and that to Dunkirk in May 1940, there was in neither case the sheltering haven of Wellington's Torres Vedras lines (1810-11). The one ended fortuitously after thirteen days in a turn of the tide; the other on the beaches in virtually the same time, the Army rescued by the Royal Navy, as at Corunna, and in addition by a fleet of little ships. It is in the early strategic moves that the similarity is most marked.

A summary of events from 24 August may help to put the Mons retreat in its right perspective. It seems almost incredible that complete destruction was avoided. Smith-Dorrien's stand at Le Cateau on the 26th, while it delayed the German advance, thus giving a breathing space in the retreat, was more significant in that he was able to break off the action in broad daylight and continue on his way even though the odds were more than two to one. It is true that von Kluck and von Bülow completely missed their opportunities, but this in no way detracts from the BEF's performance.

The original plan of envelopment was defeated when von Kluck, after his unfortunate change of direction in an attempt to cut off the French Fifth Army from the Marne, once more met the BEF, still a formidable fighting force. The Germans lost more time and the Fifth Army was saved once again. Joffre was thus able to prepare his counterstroke. When that attack came the BEF helped to save

Maunoury by being the first of the Allied forces to cross the Marne in pursuit of the Germans, and was therefore the chief factor in forcing them back to the line of the Aisne. The story has been retold here in brief because, of course, these events should never have happened.

After the Franco-Prussian War von Moltke the Elder realised the importance of military organisation in peacetime, for he saw that a nation so organised could gain such a start on her opponents that the time lost by them could never be made good. Careful strategic planning was the essential and a special organisation must be created for that purpose; thus the great German general staff came into being. Once that organisation was understood it needed no Napoleon to control it – anyone of quite ordinary capacity could be in charge provided he knew how to make use of it. In August 1914 it was planning and organisation that gave the Germans their early superiority.

It is true that a general staff had been created in England in 1904, but its proper function was not really understood, so the opinions of individuals were still placed above the collective opinion of a highly trained organisation. In this case, the individual opinion was that of a smooth-talking Irishman, Wilson, influenced by a forceful Frenchman, Foch.

Their combined opinion was wrong. The BEF walked into a trap and was forced to walk far and fast in the other direction to get out of it. Kitchener was right: concentration should have been much farther back, probably at Amiens as he had advocated. In this way the 'limited liability' of the BEF could have best been exploited and would not have suffered from the withdrawal of Lanrezac and his Fifth Army.

The foregoing is probably the most significant point for comparison with the early situation in World War II. Between the wars France constructed the Maginot Line, a series of fortifications of immense strength but of little value since a dangerous gap existed in front of the Ardennes, hilly wooded country wrongly supposed to be impracticable for the rapid movement of armour. The crossing of the Meuse at Sedan, a name of ill-omen to the French, was made by Guderian's panzers on 13 May 1940. This surprise move gave as great a shock to the world as did the violation of Belgian neutrality in 1914.

Both these far-reaching events should have been anticipated by the Allies, due to two remarkably similar circumstances. As has already been said a German staff officer defected to the French in 1904 and gave them the details of the Schlieffen Plan. In January 1940 a German aeroplane had to make a forced landing in Belgium, the pilot having lost his way in bad weather. The passenger, again a staff officer, carried with him invasion plans for the Western Front. In both cases these events were regarded with deep suspicion by the Allies as being plants, or were simply ignored. The information contained in the papers salvaged from the plane in 1940 was very similar to the Schlieffen Plan, and could very probably have been countered by the Allies since it more or less conformed to Franco-British ideas of what to expect. Why then should it have been thought to have been plant, and if it was, why was no alternative invasion route foreseen?

The new German plan, made as result of the accident, concentrated the main attack through the Ardennes which, as has already been said, was considered by the French as unsuitable for rapid movement, especially of armour. The French plan, called Plan D, was to a great extent similar to Plan XVII especially in the result since as in 1914 the BEF concentrated too far forward and thus fell into a trap; in 1940 the mad Allied rush into Belgium the moment the Germans moved played right into their hands since by coming through the Ardennes the entire German tank force outflanked the main Franco-British force and only met with inferior French formations. As in 1914, with the rapid capture of Liège and Namur due to the Austrian siege guns, and, at Liège, to Ludendorff's dynamic leadership, so once again in 1940 it was with the capture of the Belgian fortress of Eben Emael, by a tiny German airborne force landing on the roof, that the main bridges over the Albert Canal were taken before they could be blown.

It must not be thought, however, that all went according to plan on the German side. Their troops were inferior in numbers to the combined Franco-British forces, and Guderian was virtually the only general who foresaw the possibilities of the breakthrough and the necessity to push forward at all costs. He was no von Kluck. Both Hitler and the higher command were taken completely by surprise at their successes, and it was with the greatest difficulty that Guderian was able to obtain consent for further rapid forward movements, for an Allied counter-attack against the exposed flank was greatly feared. Here surely is the 'old' versus the 'new'; the old ideas of 1914-18 still persisted on both sides, while the new ideas, as personified in Guderian, triumphed because they *were* new.

143

The fear of the counter-attack, so successful in 1914, still filled the minds of the German high command with foreboding. The gains made in the early stages in 1914 due to good management, and in 1940 due to good luck, threw the opposition into confusion. In 1914 the situation was saved; in 1940 it resulted in the fall of France and the drama of the Dunkirk evacuation. On 21 May a British counter-attack at Arras took place with an armoured force far weaker than intended. This counterstroke, if it can be so called, might perhaps be compared with Lanrezac's effort at Guise. Both failed for lack of proper support, although in 1940 the Germans were still gripped by fears of the danger of their armour being unsupported by infantry. Had a really concerted effort been made by far more Allied infantry and armour combined, it is possible that a very definite check to the German advance might have been made, but it is highly improbable that the real momentum could have been halted.

The situation in Belgium, both civil and military, had got so beyond control that King Leopold capitulated with his army on 28 May, leaving the BEF, although warned, with that flank completely exposed; a not unfamiliar situation. It would be idle in 1986 to go further into all the recriminations that resulted in the nine-day evacuation at Dunkirk and the fall of France less than three weeks later. A total of 225,680 British troops were transported by various means back to England together with 322 guns, 5272 vehicles and motorcycles and 65,434 tons of petrol, ammunition and stores. It should not be forgotten that a total of 112,546 Allied troops, mostly French, were also saved by the efforts of the Royal Navy and the so famous 'little ships'; of at least 1210 Allied vessels employed, 243 were sunk. The second BEF left behind 2342 guns, 84,427 vehicles, 657,566 tons of petrol, ammunition and stores; as well as 6400 anti-tank rifles, 11,000 machine-guns and 90,000 rifles.

As in 1914, both Allies blamed each other. In the First War Sir John French saw salvation only in a retirement behind the Seine; Lord Gort, in the Second, saw it in evacuation from 19 May, very early on. The French Army in both wars was not what it was made out to be. The shadow of Napoleon fades too slowly. The French defeat lay not so much in Maginot-mindedness but, again as in 1914, in abortive ideas of attack. When in 1940 these were frustrated there was a deep fear that *nous sommes trahis* ('we are betrayed'), not only from a lack of enthusiasm for the war, but also from a deeply ingrained habit of looking over their shoulders in suspicion of political wickedness in high places; all ably abetted by skilful German propaganda.

Of the military leaders, both French and Gort were soldiers' generals, but of completely different character. 'Fat Boy' Gort, a 1918 Guards VC of outstanding courage, and a fanatic for physical fitness, had probably, like French, not enough imagination for high command in a world war. He was luckier than French in the loyalty of his subordinates. Of his corps commanders, Alanbrooke was destined later to become one of the war's outstanding figures as Churchill's mentor, a sufficiently daunting task in itself without the added responsibilities of being CIGS. Dill, the CIGS before, and less fortunate than Alanbrooke, became worn out by overwork. He was to die in Washington in 1944 when British Military Representative, and as a loved and respected figure was buried in Arlington National Cemetery – an honour accorded even to few Americans. Alexander, the *beau idéal* of a general officer, could be completely trusted to do all that it was possible to do, and took over with conspicuous success during Dunkirk when Gort was recalled to England by the Government. Bernard Law Montgomery, then a divisional commander, was also to be heard of again.

How is it possible to compare the ordinary soldiers of 1914 and 1940? First of all, it must be remembered that in 1940 there was a tail far in excess of what was needed in 1914 to get one man into the fighting line. This tail is always a problem in a retreat, as the Western Desert campaign was to show.

Among fighting troops there are always good and not so good, almost invariably a question of good or bad officers. There is the well-known story of how Tom Bridges, already mentioned as having commanded the cavalry squadron which fired the first British Army shots of the 1914 war, rallied two battalions lying, as they thought, exhausted in the streets of Valenciennes, by beating a toy drum, his trumpeter playing a penny whistle. Their commanding officers, in collaboration with the mayor, had agreed, in view of the Germans' imminent arrival, to declare Valenciennes an open town and surrender. Bridges, by his inspired leadership, saved the men. The two COs were cashiered and lucky not to have been shot. Of one it must be said that he joined the French Foreign Legion, was decorated for gallantry, and was later reinstated in the British Army. The other retired into obscurity and, it is supposed, was called up later under conscription

There are countless other stories from both retreats of lucky escapes, small parties of 'lost' soldiers being banded together by some enterprising officer or NCO and turning up again with their units. But to attempt to discriminate between the quality of the troops in the two retreats would not only be invidious but also unprofitable, in view of the two completely different outcomes, both fortunately allowing survival to fight another day. One army, alas, fought again too soon, the other at a later and more auspicious time.

In considering British retreats, the sobering thought arises as to what would have happened without the work of the Royal Navy, which has played such a vital part in many rescue operations. Exterior lines, as they are called, have many times shown the value of an island base protected by a dominant naval force. Interior lines possessed by France and Germany, which depended on the efficiency of the railway systems leading to their respective frontiers, may aid rapid mobilisation and strategic moves, but when trouble comes the possibility of an eventual getaway is greatly limited. Russia was the notable exception to efficient interior lines, her railways being inadequate for her mobilisation needs, a fact which was appreciated in one aspect of the Schlieffen Plan. It is possible that they still are, hence her reliance on East Germany.

Exterior lines depend on sea power, which has not always been appreciated by Continental Europe. Napoleon never understood such implications, but Grand Admiral Alfred von Tirpitz, Imperial Germany's Secretary of State for the Navy, produced as early as 1897 a programme of naval construction to rival that of England which met with his master the Kaiser's complete approval, but which proved to be one of the basic causes of the war. 'Rule Britannia' and 'Thank God we've got a Navy' were the constant war cries of the British people; they were also those of the United States, since much of her power was built up under Royal Navy protection. From the British point of view this feeling was well justified, since history had proved the importance of a strong fleet not only to protect their shores, but also to extricate their soldiers from trouble.

In spite of the Churchill dictum about losing the war in an afternoon, the Royal Navy did obtain strategical successes at the start of World War I: first by its early concentration in Scapa Flow after the July 1914 Fleet Review at Spithead; second in the safe transport of the BEF to France; and last by the raid into Heligoland Bight on 28 August 1914. These moves effectively frightened the German High Seas Fleet so that, until the Battle of Jutland on 31 May 1916 and the unlimited U-boat warfare of 1917, the Royal Navy did remain the mistress of the seas. And it may certainly be argued that, since the German Fleet never engaged in further action, Jutland was a tactical defeat but a strategical success.

In comparing once more the two retreats, it might appear that the Navy had nothing to do with that from Mons, since the Marne avoided the painful necessity of a rescue operation. It is well to remember, however, that during the retreat French wished to withdraw behind the Seine to rest and refit the BEF, and its bases were to be removed from Boulogne and Le Havre to St Nazaire. What perhaps is little known is that both stores and reinforcements were indeed transferred to that Atlantic port during what may be described as the 'flap'. Thus the bases were temporarily changed, which move could not have been successfully completed without the protection of the Royal Navy. It is worth noting that in June 1940 214,000 Allied troops and other personnel were evacuated from Cherbourg, St Nazaire and France's other Atlantic ports, even after Dunkirk, in the ten days prior to the ceasefire.

Dunkirk is, of course, another story. The evacuation could never have taken place without the Navy and the little ships, and also, as is so often asserted, the co-operation of Herr Hitler. It is richly ironic that he visited Dunkirk and the World War I Messines Ridge battlefield as early as 26 June 1940, the day after the ceasefire in France. Like the Kaiser, Hitler had a love-hate relationship with England, and hoped by staying his hand to bring the war to a victorious end for Germany but without great loss of face to the British people.

XV

WHY NOT PEACE 1914?

The glory has now finally departed from war, if ever there truly was any. While acknowledging the folly of jobbing backwards, always an unprofitable occupation, it may perhaps be forgiven if a study of the might-have-been is made, provided the dangers of false premise are freely admitted.

The alternatives are obvious. The first is that, had the Germans taken Paris and Channel ports, would the Allies have capitulated? The second is that, since neither of these objectives were captured, should the Germans have realised that the war was lost and given up the struggle against the considerably greater odds which were then developing? It would perhaps be best to take the second might-have-been first.

The importance of the Kaiser must be neither under- or over-estimated. British caricaturists made out that he and his son, 'Little Willie', were figures of fun, but while his posturings often made him look ridiculous, his political power was considerable, since from the very declaration of war he had managed to unite all the parties in Germany in a common effort. As the 'All Highest War Lord', he had according to tradition moved his HQ alongside those of the great general staff, first to Coblenz, then Luxembourg, and later to Charleville-Mézières. In spite of this nearness to von Moltke and, afterwards, to Falkenhayn he was, much to his chagrin, not consulted in military matters by either commander, although he was instrumental in the removal of von Moltke and the appointment of his successor Falkenhayn.

The failure of the Germans to gain a rapid victory, and especially the failures before Nancy and Ypres, where he had been present to act the conquering hero, had saddened the Kaiser. On the question of a settlement with the Allies he had certain definite ideas: first, an early peace with Russia and then a quick ending of the whole war, since he feared the effect on the civilian population of heavy casualties and the Allied blockade. His son the Crown Prince, an army commander, was more definite: 'We have lost the war. It will go on for a long time but it is already lost.'

Quite apart from the military and political aspects of the situation, there was a dynastic link.

The Kaiser, it must not be forgotten, was the grandson of Queen Victoria, and although she was at times apt to treat him as the naughty small boy which he often closely resembled, he regarded her with a mixture of awe and affection. Uncle Bertie, Edward VII, was an entirely different proposition. The Kaiser was both jealous and envious of him which resulted in a mutual dislike – this showed in various forms, especially in the rivalry during Cowes Week between the two monarchs' yachts. A German once remarked that 'you English will always be fools but we Germans will never be gentlemen'. The Kaiser's dearest wish was to be thought a 'gentleman', and for this reason he often rented English country houses for quite long periods, during which time he played the squire.

There was thus a love-hate relationship between the Emperor and England, the hate side coming to the fore after, as he considered, Britain's completely unnecessary declaration of war. In 1914 the Kaiser's mind, in spite of the war, held firm to the relationship of the three reigning first cousins William, George and Nicholas. He reckoned that, blood being thicker than water, the three emperors could, when the right time came, settle the affair between them. They did not need some upstart president like Woodrow Wilson to meddle in a business which did not concern him.

As will be seen later, such support as a peace plan put forward by the Kaiser might have had in Britain was largely negated by propaganda and German 'frightfulness' in Belgium. 'The most brilliant failure in history', as Edward VII described his nephew, had by a blunder worse than a crime aided and abetted his country into a war which she could never win; having done so, he lacked the authority, however much he really wished to do so, to make peace on any other terms than his own. In spite of efforts made by neutral royalty, of which more will be heard later, there was no real hope of peace with England through the Kaiser. What other avenues then were open? The German people, used to the arrogance of the military, were waiting hopefully to see whether their subservience would be justified by great military successes, but there was little hope of the emergence of any strong peace party, especially in view of the Kaiser's success in uniting all political factions.

The only possible way open was through the German Army. Flushed with the early successes, its leaders, with the exception of von Moltke, all seemed to bear the subsequent retreat with considerable fortitude, on the assumption that it was merely a question of '*reculer pour mieux sauter*' ('retiring the better to recover'). Von Moltke, however, thought differently, to him 'the terrible difficulty of our situation often stands like a black wall in front of me, seeming quite impenetrable'. By then he was a sick man. What the Crown Prince thought has already been quoted, but the other princelings, probably fearful for their jobs both military and royal, would advocate the continuation of the war as their only means of salvation. The lesser army commanders most of whom heartily disliked each other either for professional or ethnic reasons, would not favour peace. They were comparatively old, and if peace was made would be both discredited and on the shelf.

A junta of more junior officers would equally be against a peace. The Army had lorded it over the civilian population for so long that some justification for the officer class was necessary, not only for social reasons but also because, as many were poor and promotion was slow, they had everything to lose. That the ordinary soldier, a highly disciplined being except when looted drink was obtainable, should consider a settlement was unthinkable. In spite of the casualties there was at this time, especially among the student element, a fanatical form of patriotism that would reappear twenty-five years later. From the German side, a negotiated peace would seem to have been out of the question. If, however, by some miracle a settlement had been arrived at, what terms would the Allies have imposed?

In the east, Germany, Austria-Hungary and Russia could probably have argued out their differences without much difficulty, since the Kaiser, as has been seen, considered a separate peace with Russia as the first possibility. Austria-Hungary was not very likely to have much stomach for the war anyway, due to her internal ethnic problems; she could easily forget that it was through those problems that the whole conflagration had been started. The Tsar, as stubborn as Charles I and Louis XVI, must even so have realised that sooner rather than later his days were numbered by revolt from within, even without the aid of such military disasters as Tannenberg.

The situation in the west was entirely different. On the Allied side it was the 'frocks' rather than the military who would have to settle the affair. A widespread loss of face would at all costs have to be avoided if a negotiated peace was to be a possibility. It must be remembered that at this early stage the war had not yet reached a point of no return; Asquith was still the Prime Minister of a Liberal Government, several of whose members had been against war from the outset.

Contrary to general belief, the British public are easily swayed in their feelings. Early enthusiasm for the war could probably have been replaced by a feeling of relief that it really was over by Christmas and that the Germans were not such bad chaps after all; no need to continue to be beastly to them. It would have needed clever propaganda, but it could have been done. Such of the old Army as were left would have felt elation that, even if the glory had departed, they had survived with credit (and great good fortune) from an extremely 'near run thing'. Friends would be sorely missed, but there was much promotion in store. Kitchener's Men would have returned to their homes, perhaps disappointed at the lack of opportunity to show their merit, but with considerable relief for their families. The generals could continue their squabbles, which they did anyway, and the 'good old days' would return once more.

France had not yet the inflexible Clemenceau, 'the Tiger', in power. She had suffered enormous casualties and was highly conscious of the value of her possessions. The most treasured, Paris, had been saved, why should further loss be suffered? Alsace and Lorraine must, of course, be returned. The damage done by 'frightfulness' to Belgium would have to be compensated. Strict limitations on the building of warships in competition with the Royal Navy must be agreed, and some limitation of armaments and forces must be imposed. The Kaiser, having learned his lesson, should not abdicate since he was certainly the best guarantee of peace for the future, or so it was hoped. All could be sweetness and light again. The British could have the Irish problem, and the Changing of the Guard in scarlet, once more, the French the constant procession of changing governments, and the Belgians the pleasure of rebuilding what had been destroyed. The only real profit-makers would be the United States, looking on with great satisfaction from the sidelines.

But what of the first alternative, a loss of Paris and, its inevitable

151

sequel, that of the Channel ports? A military situation which might bring about these two catastrophes need not be gone into, since it very nearly came about. Paris is a very sensitive chink in the French armour. In 1870–71 she had put up a more than stubborn defence. In 1914 she would also have done so, but it is assumed for the purpose of this exercise that she would have fallen, taking into account the power of the new siege guns so effective against Liège and Namur. In 1940 Paris was declared an open city after the government left it for Tours and then Bordeaux (as in 1914), but her occupation and the colossal exodus of all but 700,000 inhabitants presaged the fall of France. Then the Army had not greatly suffered in killed and wounded, but in 1914 the casualties were horrific and, under the circumstances here presented, France's leaders would have been completely disgraced, with only very few exceptions. The survivors would not have been strong enough to rally a mistrusted government and a defeated army. Under such circumstances, it is almost a certainty that France would have sued for peace.

If this great disaster had occurred, what would Britain have done? (It can be assumed that the Channel ports would also have been lost.) Any concentration of the BEF behind the Seine, as was planned by French early in the retreat, or his later idea of an entrenched camp round Boulogne, would have been useless in view of the collapse of the French Army. Admittedly, the Boulogne project might have been used as a rearguard position for the embarkation of such of the British Army as survived. However, since Winston Churchill had not guaranteed the safety of the BEF crossing, and if, at the beginning of the war, Antwerp had been decided on as the concentration area, it was quite possible that German naval attempts to disrupt the safe passage of the survivors might have resulted in a full-scale sea battle. It was Winston Churchill who said that the war could be lost in an afternoon. An earlier Jutland might have done just that, for the vulnerability of the battle-fleet, fortunately, did not become evident until 1916.

The divided feeling in the British Cabinet has already been mentioned, but would the general public have accepted such an ignominious defeat? Asquith was hardly a rallying force, but could Lloyd George have done what Churchill did in 1940? The BEF, it would have been said, had been defeated due to the incapacity of its leaders. Of course, the French would have had to bear a large part of the

152

blame for 'letting the side down', while in France 'Perfide Albion' would have had the same treatment. At this stage of the war Britain was in no position to resist invasion. The 'I was playing golf the day that the Germans landed' mentality, combined with 'business as usual', hardly helped the populace towards a determination to resist, especially since the old regulars were no more and Kitchener's Army was still untrained. The only hope would have been Kitchener. His immense popularity and prestige might have been strong enough to rouse a still lethargic populace, and since, as is now known, invasion takes an unconscionable time to mount, his army might have been capable of meeting such a threat, having had more time to train.

The Kaiser, like Hitler in 1940, had a weakness where Britain was concerned. Cousin does not eat cousin, and peace terms might not have been as onerous as might be thought. But Germany would have become the dominant force in Europe, with Britain unable to maintain the balance of power, since in no way could naval parity be accepted. It would be idle to speculate on colonial concessions, but inevitably there would have been a definite policy of weakening Great Britain as a world power. France would have suffered another huge indemnity and the continued loss of Alsace and Lorraine, while further frontier trimming would have been inevitable in order that Germany might consolidate her new triumphs.

There would have been little change in the east. Russia was still a force to be reckoned with, but once more the cousins might have come to an amicable frontier alignment. Austria-Hungary, under the aged Francis Joseph, was so debilitated by her internal and Balkan problems that she was in no position to argue with her powerful ally regarding any terms of peace, and would simply have had to do what she was told by Germany.

What conclusions can be drawn from what might be considered to be mere idle speculation? The answer, of course, is more idle speculation. In the first place, if the Germans had realised the futility of continuing the war the terms of peace would have been conducted far more by negotiation than was the case once she had lost. It must be remembered that when a boxer loses a fight his first thought is for a return match – so it is with nations. From 1870 to 1914 is forty-four years, 1918 to 1939 is only twenty-one; what period of peace could have been forecast? Possibly thirty years since there would have been no pressure from a Versailles treaty or an economic collapse. The nations at war would have been spared the casualties and the appalling wastage caused by war.

It was King Farouk of Egypt who said that in future there would only be five kings left; the kings of spades, hearts, diamonds, clubs, and the King of England. Autocratic monarchy, even in 1914, was a dying institution. How long could the Kaiser and the Crown Prince have lasted in Germany? At all events, Germany, Europe and the United States would have been spared Hitler. The Austro-Hungarian Empire would probably have disintegrated after Francis Joseph and, as has already been said, Czar Nicholas II had outlived his time.

The foregoing are admittedly all rhetorical questions. What follows are definite ideas, which, it is hoped, will in some way justify speculation that a definite peace overture was possible in 1914, provided it was pursued with energy. Such speculation is not already understood, will perhaps be made clearer if the political and military situations inside Germany are appreciated.

If the agony columns of newspapers are to be believed (and indeed the reports of people's deaths are seldom exaggerated), there is today a surplus of the aged. The events covered by this book took place just over seventy years ago, but there is still a large number of eighty- and ninety-year-olds who at least remember, some perhaps only vaguely, those grim and fateful times. The Second World War has possibly obliterated the memory of the First so far as the middle-aged are concerned, and to the young both wars, if they think about them at all, are 'old, unhappy, far-off things, And battles long ago'.

It is almost incredible, therefore, that a dynastic war has been fought in the memory of many living today; perhaps even a mediaeval war. This contention is only strictly true, however, in the case of Germany and Russia. As has already been seen, the Kaiser only considered the possibility of treating for peace with rulers, all of whom were closely related to each other. While perhaps not popular with everyone, interference today by the President of the United States, in no matter what important event taking place in the world, is nevertheless inevitable. In 1914 he was considered to be a meddling *parvenu*; not so even by 1918, nor, indeed, ever since.

In 1914 the German field armies were led as a matter of course by the princes of the federated states, in spite of the so-called united German

Empire. In the Middle Ages also, armies were led by rulers or their sons. Admittedly some of the German princes had military advisers but one, the forty-five-year-old Prince Rupert of Bavaria, was a 'highly competent commander of the northern army group' on the Western Front. He was 'dismayed to find the All Highest War Lord [Kaiser William II] a puppet of the supreme command: he had been surprised when the Kaiser on 22 December 1917 inspected troops in the Cambrai-Le Cateau area and brought them greetings and praise from the Field-Marshal [Hindenburg]. It worried Rupert that a sovereign should thus appear the mouthpiece of a subject before his troops: "In the old days it would have been impossible," Rupert commented.' (Quoted from Alan Palmer's 1977 biography of the Kaiser.)

The First World War, it may be stated categorically, was of greater historical importance than the Second for a number of reasons. First, if either side had sued for peace there would have been no Hitler, whatever may have been the cause of his rise to power, and therefore no war. Second, since the Great War took its full course, the outcome did result in a second war. In both cases World War I was the dominating factor.

The Germans today feel a deep guilt about the Nazis, but they do not perhaps realise the part played by Bismarck in 1870 and the Kaiser in 1914 in the attempts to humiliate first France and then England. The 1914-18 War saw the end of the great Central and East European dynasties. Today, seventy years on, there is still a sovereign in this country and Belgium, a president of the United States, a president of France and a communist Russia, as there were in 1939. There is also, it must not be forgotten, a divided Germany.

To turn back once more to the question of peace overtures, these, such as they were, were to be all dynastic and, according to the Kaiser, largely depended on the attitude of Nicholas II of Russia. There were, however, dynastic links between Bavaria and Belgium which might also have been used to influence King Albert I of the Belgians. The principal contact, setting aside the relationship between the two rulers, was through the Grand Duke of Hesse, whose sister was the Russian Empress Alexandra: nothing seems to have come of this.

The main move towards direct contact with Russia was made through King Christian X of Denmark, which, although begun in November 1914, continued until August 1915. The King of Denmark's suggestion that an industrialist, Hans Niels Andersen, should approach England was turned down by William, but the Czar was considered to be a definite possibility. Nicholas was not unsympathetic, but characteristically delayed giving any definite answer. Eventually the possible capture of Constantinople as a result of the Gallipoli landings so elated the Czar that when the answer did come it was negative. It is a strange coincidence that similar moves were made by a Swedish industrialist (Birger Dahlerus) at the beginning of World War II, and with the same result, this time in view of the overpowering German successes.

XVI

EPILOGUE

... The Captains and the Kings depart:
Still stands Thine ancient sacrifice
An humble and a contrite heart.

'Recessional' *Rudyard Kipling*

Although the departure of the kings was not yet to be, that of the captains, either into obscurity or to other spheres of activity, was either imminent or in the not-so-distant future. The fates of the principal protagonists in the drama already unfolded are of considerable interest due to their very diversity; they cannot all be dismissed with a short footnote. The 'frocks' must also be included, since they had such a disproportionate influence over the military in the conduct of a war.

Von Moltke has already gone, a victim of a 'humble and a contrite heart'. He was to die in 1916, probably a sadder and a wiser man than all the others. What a pity that, unlike von Rundstedt on 1 July 1944, he had not the courage to say 'make peace, you fools'.

First Ypres was no château-directed battle. Sadly, as has already been told, Lomax and Monro, two divisional commanders, were casualties as a result of the shelling at Hooge. Hubert Hamilton, commanding the 3rd Division, was killed on 14 October; FitzClarence, commanding the 1st Guards Brigade, was also killed when organising a counter-attack. More than fifty staff officers were killed, belying a popular belief that they were not to be found at the front line.

Both French and Haig had been prepared to immolate themselves on the altar of sacrifice; French being deterred by the timely intervention of Foch, and Haig by the charge of the Worcesters at Gheluvelt. These, however, were the happenings of the moment. What then did the future hold for the principals, among many of whom feelings of 'a humble and a contrite heart' were conspicuous by their absence?

157

Of those who had attended the Downing Street conference on 5 August, Lieutenant-General Sir James Grierson was of course the first to die. This was unfortunate, since he was probably the ablest of them all. (After receiving the RFC airship *Gamma*'s radio reports in the August 1912 Army manoeuvres he had spoken of a revolution in the art of war, and predicted that the first step in war would be to 'get rid' of hostile aircraft.) He himself had realised that a mixture of hard work and good living was not conducive to a long life.

In November 1914 Field-Marshal Lord Roberts, the senior officer in the British Army, although well into his eighties had determined to visit his beloved Indian troops (3rd Lahore and 7th Meerut Divisions) suffering severely under the appalling conditions imposed on them by a Flanders winter since coming into the line on 23 October to relieve II Corps. The 4th Battalion, 10th Baluch Regiment fired the Indian Corps' first infantry shots on 31 October, and its machine-gunners were cut off that day. That detachment's sole survivor won the first of five VCs awarded to Indian troops in France. Accompanied by his daughter Aileen, the Field-Marshal carried out a rigorous schedule, to the delight of so many whose fathers had served under him. He caught a chill and died at St Omer on 15 November. He had been much pleased that the Colonelcy-in-Chief of the Imperial troops had been conferred on him by Lord Kitchener as a sop to a more active command. Sir Pertab Singh, wearing a greatcoat lent him by the Prince of Wales, accompanied the coffin to England. For a Rajput prince thus to lose caste was perhaps the greatest honour of all those paid to a greatly loved figure. The Indian Corps remained in France till the end of 1915 before joining the other Indian Army formations in the war with Turkey.

The next to go, perhaps the greatest of all in the eyes of most people then, was Kitchener of Khartoum, the 'War Lord', for thus he had become to the discomfiture of the Government and those responsible for the conduct of the war in the field. On 5 June 1916 the cruiser HMS *Hampshire* struck a mine off the Shetlands when taking him to Russia, where it was hoped that he might do something to rally a rapidly deteriorating situation. 'K' was not among the twelve survivors. Much was made of so-called mysteries surrounding the sinking of the large cruiser and the real circumstances would still seem to be unresolved to this day. He was greatly mourned by the nation, but not by the

Government or by his friends for, as it was said, he had none.

Another to die in 1916 was Gallieni, the governor of Paris at the time of the 'turn of the tide'. He is of course chiefly remembered for the taxi-cabs commandeered to rush troops from Paris to the front, but he subsequently became minister of war and was a severe critic of Joffre, to whom he was senior, as he also was to Foch. They had both been promoted over his head. He received a posthumous marshal's baton in 1921, hardly compensation for dying from overwork in 1916.

All the captains were shortly to depart to other spheres. Rather obviously, the first to go was Smith-Dorrien, 'The Man Who Disobeyed', particularly as a result of Le Cateau. He and French were at daggers drawn. After the shocking casualties suffered in the counter-attacks following the German gas attack in the Second Battle of Ypres in the spring of 1915, Smith-Dorrien proposed to straighten the 'salient' to stop further heavy losses. The net result was that he was ordered to hand over Second Army to Lieutenant-General Sir Herbert Plumer, and was to hear over the telephone from Sir William Robertson the already quoted words "'Orace you're for 'Ome". Like many others Sir Horace paid the penalty for being right, but the true irony lay in the fact that the very withdrawal he proposed, and for which he was sacked, was later ordered by Plumer. In the 1920s a film was made of the Retreat from Mons and in it Smith-Dorrien played himself, surely both the first and last general to do so. He was to die in 1930.

Much has already been written about both Sir John French and Sir Douglas Haig. In December 1915 French, after much intrigue against him, not always unjustified, was succeeded as Commander-in-Chief by his chief detractor, Sir Douglas Haig. The main reason put forward, however, was French's handling of the Battle of Loos, in which the 'New Armies' (Kitchener's Army) suffered from bad staffwork and from lack of training. French became Commander-in-Chief Home Forces and later, during 1918-21, Lord Lieutenant of Ireland, where he seems to have handled an extremely difficult situation with some success. He was created Earl of Ypres, and died in 1925. He remained ever-popular with the troops, if not with a large number of husbands.

Of Sir Douglas Haig, so much has been written by so many, and his portrayal so often distorted by those making a cheap jibe or an expensive film, that perhaps no further comment is needed here since, in the compass of this work, Haig's I Corps did not play an overprominent part until First Ypres. He survived as Commander-in-Chief, in spite of the efforts of Lloyd George to unseat him, until the end of the war. Created Earl Haig of Bermersyde he died in 1928 and is commemorated in Whitehall by perhaps the worst statue in London, of which Lady Haig is reported to have said 'my husband never rode a cart horse'. His greatest memorial is the Earl Haig Fund for old soldiers – today The Royal British Legion – brought every year to public notice around 11 November (Armistice Day) by what is commonly called 'Poppy Day'.

'Wully' Robertson, who had become French's Chief of Staff, left at the same time as his master to become CIGS. The private had at last become the field-marshal. Robertson had succeeded Sir Archibald Murray as Chief of Staff when the latter was sacked by French in typically devious circumstances, although French had slighted Robertson to such an extent that they did not even share the same mess. Robertson in his turn, owing to differences with Lloyd George, was succeeded in 1918 by no less a figure than Sir Henry Wilson. So the political dance went on, which well suited Henry Wilson, of whom it was said 'He got into a state of sexual excitement whenever he saw a politician.'

Robertson was to die in 1933, Henry Wilson in June 1922, shot by the Irish outside his London home in Eaton Place when returning from an investiture. He died with sword in his hand, the last field-marshal to do so.

Of the original BEF generals, Allenby and Rawlinson were perhaps the most successful. Sir Henry Rawlinson, together with Haig, takes the credit for the conception of the attack before Amiens on 8 August 1918 which Ludendorff described as 'the Black Day of the German Army'. Rawlinson was later to become Commander-in-Chief in India, but died very suddenly in 1933 after a polo match. Sir Edmund Allenby, known as the 'Bull', was perhaps the most colourful figure of all. After his successful handling of the Cavalry Division during the retreat he had limited success as commander of the Third Army in France. His claim to fame rests on the 1917-18 campaign in Palestine. This culminated, in September and October 1918, with a surprise due to a deception plan and the cutting of the enemy communications by the Royal Air Force which enabled brilliant cavalry sweeps to brush aside Turkish opposition. The result was an advance of 350 miles in thirty-eight days and the capture of 75,000 prisoners. The Arabs, under the Emir Feisal, subsidised by British gold generously handed out by T.E. Lawrence (he is still known as 'the man with the money') helped by cutting railway lines and making a general nuisance of themselves to the Turks, and also occasionally to their paymasters. The conception of this great strategic move was all Allenby's, and his biography by Field-Marshal Earl Wavell (certainly the most intellectual if not the greatest general of World War II) is a classic of its kind.

After the war, Allenby had marked success as High Commissioner in Egypt, surprising in a man of such autocratic and sometimes violent temperament, and was instrumental in giving that frustrated country nominal autonomy in 1922. Megiddo and Felixstowe were a rather startling combination for his title of Viscount; perhaps the 'Bull' had a sense of humour after all. He was to die in retirement in 1936.

Of the French, Lanrezac was the first among many to go, a notable example of strategical ability on paper and tactical failure in the field. Joffre survived the casualties of Verdun and the Somme gradually to be eased out with a marshal's baton and other sops not entailing executive command. Taking the hint, he retired in favour of General Robert Nivelle at the end of 1916. The latter's disastrous apointment triggered off the April 1917 mutinies in the French Army which were controlled so ably by General Henri Philippe Pétain, who in 1940, as Head of the Vichy Government, became the arch-collaborator with the Germans. Joffre died in 1931.

Much has already been written about Foch and his influence over Sir John French and his friendship with Sir Henry Wilson. In May 1918, after the German breakthrough of March that year, he took over the supreme command in France as Allied Generalissimo. With the possible exception of Haig he is probably the general best remembered today, since it was he, after all, who held the chief command when the Armistice with Germany was signed on 11 November 1918 in a railway carriage in the Forest of Compiègne. He died in 1929 and in England is commemorated by an equestrian statue outside Victoria Station (a copy of the statue that stands at Cassel, his HQ for Ypres) much used by the local pigeons, although not always as a vantage point from which to survey the travellers arriving from the Continent.

Of the soldiers, only the Germans are now left. Von Kluck may not have been a great general but he was a brave old man, having been wounded when visiting the front line in 1915. As a veteran of the Prussian wars against the Austrians and the French he must have been pretty tough since, even though wounded aged seventy, he did not die until 1934. Von Bülow retained command of the Second Army throughout the war without particular distinction, probably aided by being a member of one of the most prominent political families.

Erich von Falkenhayn (1861-1922) kept his post until after his abortive and costly attacks on Verdun in 1916. Then in December he was succeeded technically by Field-Marshal Paul von Hindenburg although, but as in many cases, it was the chief of staff who did the real work; in this instance Erich von Ludendorff, to whom the 'von' had been granted for services rendered. After his distinguished war career Ludendorff disappeared to Sweden, following the Armistice. Feeling betrayed and misunderstood he strayed into National Socialism and was arrested after Hitler's Munich *Putsch* in 1923. He was released, but kept close contact with Hitler during 1924-28, even standing for the Chancellorship against his old chief Hindenburg. He was not a particularly engaging figure, although his later involvement with Nazism disguises his genius as a staff officer. He died in 1937.

Of the politicians, Haldane was certainly the most shamefully treated. Probably the greatest and most far-seeing of all war ministers, he was hounded out of office by the baying of the press and public because he was once supposed to have said that Germany was his spiritual home. Similarly, there was no more loyal servant of the Crown than Prince Louis of Battenberg, who had become First Sea Lord in 1914. He too was said because of his name to have German sympathies. He was obliged to resign and changed his name to Mountbatten, one to be borne with considerable distinction by his son.

Herbert Henry Asquith (First Earl of Oxford), the Prime Minister at the beginning of the war, a strange, whimsical, intellectual figure, was hardly fitted to be the principal statesman of a great empire in a great war. He certainly was, with the exception of Kitchener, the only member of the Cabinet to foresee a long war; even Sir Edward Grey, the Foreign Secretary, subscribed to the 'over by Christmas' fallacy. Asquith was unfortunately a man of intemperate habits and his inability even in writing to keep secret information from his intimates, together with the verbal indiscretions of his wife Margot, whose autobiography caused a sensation after the war, must have been a sore trial to his fellow ministers. He was succeeded as Prime Minister in December 1916 by Lloyd George but continued to be leader of a declining Liberal Party until 1926. He died in 1928.

Lloyd George's period of office does not come within the scope of this work,but it is an interesting sidelight on the times how these two men were able to hold high office in view of their disorganised private lives. Such would have been impossible even thirty years earlier, as witness Charles Parnell and Sir Charles Dilke, and that would also appear to be so today.

What of those who have not entered the hall of fame or of infamy? The trumpets may have sounded for them on the other side, but here they are commemorated either in beautifully kept cemeteries literally alas 'row on row', or on such memorials as the Menin Gate at Ypres dedicated to those who have no known grave. The greatest hope is that 'their bodies are buried in peace', but it is perhaps more important that 'Their name liveth for evermore'.

Appendix A

KITCHENER'S INSTRUCTIONS TO SIR JOHN FRENCH, C-IN-C BEF, AUGUST 1914

The special motive of the Force under your control is to support and co-operate with the French Army against our common enemies [Author's italics]. The peculiar task laid upon you is to assist the French Government in preventing or repelling the invasion by Germany of French and Belgian territory and eventually to restore the neutrality of Belgium, on behalf of which, as guaranteed by treaty, Belgium has appealed to the French and to ourselves.

These are the reasons which have induced His Majesty's Government to declare war, and these reasons constitute the primary objective you have before you.

The place of your assembly, according to present arrangements, is Amiens [*sic*], and during the assembly of your troops you will have every opportunity for discussing with the Commander-in-Chief of the French Army, the military position in general and the special part which your Force is able and adapted to play. It must be recognised from the outset that the numerical strength of the British Force and its contingent reinforcement is strictly limited, and with this consideration kept steadily in view it will be obvious that the greatest care must be exercised towards a minimum of losses and wastage.

Therefore, while every effort must be made to coincide most sympathetically with the plans and wishes of our ally, the gravest consideration will devolve upon you as to participation in forward movements where large bodies of French troops are not engaged and where your Force may be unduly exposed to attack. Should a contingency of this sort be contemplated, *I look to you to inform me fully and give me time to communicate to you any decision to which His Majesty's*

Government may come in the matter [Author's italics]. In this connection I wish you distinctly to understand that your command is an entirely independent one, and that you will in no case come in any sense under the orders of any Allied General.

In minor operations you should be careful that your subordinates understand that risk of serious losses should only be taken where such risk is authoritatively considered to be commensurate with the object in view.

The high courage and discipline of your troops should, and certainly will, have fair and full opportunity of display during the campaign, but officers may well be reminded that in this, their first experience of European warfare, a greater measure of caution must be employed than under former conditions of hostilities against an untrained adversary.

You will kindly keep up constant communication with the War Office, and you will be good enough to inform me as to all movements of the enemy reported to you as well as to those of the French Army.

I am sure you fully realise that you can rely with the utmost confidence on the wholehearted and unswerving support of the Government, of myself, and of your compatriots, in carrying out the high duty which the King has entrusted to you and in maintaining the great tradition of His Majesty's Army.

(Signed) KITCHENER,
Secretary of State

Appendix B

THE BEF ORDER OF BATTLE
August–November 1914

GENERAL HEADQUARTERS

Commander-in-Chief: Field-Marshal Sir J.D.P. French GCB, GCVO, KCMG
Chief of the General Staff: Lt-Gen Sir A.J. Murray KCB, CVO, DSO
Major-General, General Staff: Maj-Gen H.H. Wilson CB, DSO
General Staff Officer I (Intelligence): Col G.M.W. Macdonogh
Adjutant-General: Maj-Gen (became Lt-Gen) Sir C.F.N. Macready
Quartermaster-General: Maj-Gen Sir W.R. Robertson KCVO, CB, DSO

CAVALRY DIVISION

Maj-Gen E.H. Allenby CB i/c Cavalry Corps as
Lt-Gen on formation on 9 October, Brig-Gen de Lisle
taking command of 1st Cavalry Division, and
Maj-Gen Gough (promoted Lt-Gen 27 Oct)
2nd Cavalry Division

1st Cavalry Brigade

(to 1st Cav Div, Oct)

Brig-Gen C.J. Briggs CB
2nd Dragoon Guards (Queen's Bays)
5th Dragoon Guards
11th Hussars

2nd Cavalry Brigade

(to 1st Cav Div, Oct)

Brig-Gen H. de B. de Lisle CB, DSO replaced by Brig-Gen R.L. Mullins (Oct)
4th Dragoon Guards
9th Lancers
18th Hussars (Queen Mary's Own)

3rd Cavalry Brigade

(to 2nd Cav Div, Oct)

Brig-Gen H. de la P. Gough CB
    replaced by Brig-Gen J. Vaughan
    DSO
4th Hussars
5th Lancers
16th Lancers

5th Cavalry Brigade

(to 2nd Cav Div, Oct)

Brig-Gen Sir P.W. Chetwode Bart,
    DSO
2nd Dragoons (Royal Scots Greys)
12th Lancers
20th Hussars

4th Cavalry Brigade

(to 2nd Cav Div, Oct)

Brig-Gen Hon C.E. Bingham CVO,
    CB
Household Cavalry Regiment*
6th Dragoon Guards (Carabiniers)
3rd Hussars
* replaced by Oxfordshire Hussars
    (11 Nov)

Royal Horse Artillery

'D', 'E', 'I', 'J', 'L' Batteries
('H' Bty replaced 'L' after Néry on 1
    Sept, arriving mid-Sept; 'D' and
    'E' Btys went to 2nd Cav Div
    then, followed by 'J' Bty in Oct)

1st-5th Cavalry Field Ambulances
1st and 2nd Divisional Supply
    Columns

Royal Engineers

1st and 2nd Field Squadrons
1st and 2nd Signal Squadrons

I CORPS

Lt-Gen Sir D. Haig KCB, KCIE, KCVO, ADC-Gen (promoted Gen
20 November)
Brigadier-General, General Staff: Brig-Gen J.E.
Gough VC, CMG, ADC

1ST DIVISION

Maj-Gen S.H. Lomax wounded as Lt-Gen 31 October, replaced by

Maj-Gen Landon (temp) and then by Maj-Gen Sir D. Henderson (from RFC).

1st (Guards) Brigade

Brig-Gen F.I. Maxse CVO, CB, DSO replaced by Brig-Gen FitzClarence VC killed 11 November. Col McEwen took command.
1st Bn Coldstream Guards
1st Bn Scots Guards
1st Bn Royal Highlanders (Black Watch)
2nd Bn Royal Munster Fusiliers (suffered severe casualties at Etreux 27 Aug replaced by 1st Bn Cameron Highlanders about 6 Sept)
London Scottish (first Territorial Force unit) joined 7 November.

3rd Infantry Brigade

Brig-Gen H.J.S. Landon CB promoted and replaced by Brig-Gen R.H.K. Butler 13 November.
1st Bn The Queen's Royal West Surrey Regiment (suffered severe casualties 31 Oct, replaced by 2nd Royal Munster Fusiliers)
1st Bn South Wales Borderers
1st Bn Welch Regiment

Royal Artillery

Col Findlay
25th Brigade (113, 114, 115 Batteries)
26th Brigade (116, 117, 118 Batteries)
39th Brigade (46, 51, 54 Batteries)

2nd Infantry Brigade

Brig-Gen E.S. Bulfin CVO, CB wounded as Lt-Gen 1 November, replaced by Col Cunliffe-Owen (temp). Brig-Gen Westmacott took command 23 November.
2nd Bn Royal Sussex Regiment
1st Bn North Lancashire Regiment
1st Bn Northamptonshire Regiment
2nd King's Royal Rifle Corps
9th Bn Highland Light Infantry (TF, from 24 Nov)

Divisional Cavalry

'C' Squadron 15th Hussars
1st Cyclist Company

Royal Engineers

23rd and 26th Field Companies
1st Signal Company

1st Divisional Train
1st, 2nd, 3rd Field Ambulances

43rd (Howitzer) Brigade (30, 40, 57 Batteries)
26th Heavy Battery, Royal Garrison Artillery

2ND DIVISION

Maj-Gen C.C. Monro CB disabled temporarily
31 October.

4th (Guards) Brigade

Brig-Gen R. Scott-Kerr CB, MVO, DSO wounded 1 September, replaced by Brig-Gen the Earl of Cavan on 18 September.
2nd Bn Grenadier Guards
2nd Bn Coldstream Guards
3rd Bn Coldstream Guards
1st Bn Irish Guards
1st Hertfordshire Regiment
(Territorial Force, joined 19 Nov)

6th Infantry Brigade

Brig-Gen R.H. Davies CB (NZ Staff Corps) invalided in September, replaced by Brig-Gen R. Fanshawe 13 September.
1st Bn King's (Liverpool) Regiment
2nd Bn South Staffordshire Regiment
1st Bn Royal Berkshire Regiment
1st Bn King's Royal Rifle Corps

Royal Artillery

Brig-Gen E.M. Perceval
34th Brigade (25, 50, 70 Batteries)
36th Brigade (15, 48, 71 Batteries)
41st Brigade (9, 16, 17 Batteries)
44th (Howitzer) Brigade (47, 56, 60 Batteries)
35th Heavy Battery, Royal Garrison Artillery

5th Infantry Brigade

Brig-Gen R.C.B. Haking CB wounded 16 September, replaced by Lt-Col Westmacott until return 20 November.
2nd Bn Worcestershire Regiment
2nd Bn Oxford & Buckinghamshire Light Infantry
2nd Bn Highland Light Infantry
2nd Bn Connaught Rangers
9th Bn Highland Light Infantry (TF, from 24 Nov)

Divisional Cavalry

'B' Squadron 15th Hussars
2nd Cyclist Company

Royal Engineers

5th and 11th Field Companies
2nd Signal Company

2nd Divisional Train
4th and 6th Field Ambulances

II CORPS

Lt-Gen Sir J.M. Grierson KCB, CVO, CMG,
ADC-Gen died 17 August.
Gen Sir H.L. Smith-Dorrien GCB, DSO
Brigadier-General, General Staff: Brig-Gen G.T.
Forestier-Walker ADC

3RD DIVISION

Maj-Gen H.I.W. Hamilton CVO, CB, DSO killed 14
October replaced by Maj-Gen C.S. Mackenzie CB
till 29 October, Maj-Gen F.D.V. Wing CB till 22
November, then Maj-Gen Haldane.

7th Infantry Brigade

Brig-Gen F.W.N. McCracken CB,
  DSO
3rd Bn Worcestershire Regiment
2nd Bn South Lancashire Regiment
1st Bn Wiltshire Regiment
2nd Bn Royal Irish Rifles

9th Infantry Brigade

Brig-Gen F.C. Shaw CB wounded
  12 November replaced by Lt-Col
  Douglas Smith (R Scots Fusiliers).
1st Bn Northumberland Fusiliers
4th Bn Royal Fusiliers
1st Bn Lincolnshire Regiment
1st Bn Royal Scots Fusiliers
10th Bn King's Regiment
  (Territorial Force, 25 Nov)

8th Infantry Brigade

Brig-Gen B.J.C. Doran CB
  invalided 23 October, replaced by
  Brig-Gen Bowes.
2nd Bn Royal Scots
2nd Bn Royal Irish Regiment (severe
  casualties at Le Pilly 20 Oct,
  became GHQ troops, replaced by
  2nd Bn Suffolk Regt)
4th Bn Middlesex Regiment
1st Bn Gordon Highlanders (GHQ
  troops during Sept, replaced by
  1st Bn Devon Regt but rejoined
  early Oct)
1st Bn Honourable Artillery
  Company (TF, 9 Nov)

Royal Artillery

Brig-Gen F.D.V. Wing
23rd Brigade (107, 108, 109
    Batteries)
40th Brigade (6, 23, 49 Batteries)
42nd Brigade (29, 41, 45 Batteries)
30th (Howitzer) Brigade (128, 129,
    130 Batteries)
48th Heavy Battery, Royal Garrison
    Artillery

Divisional Cavalry

'A' Squadron 15th Hussars
3rd Cyclist Company

Royal Engineers

56th and 57th Field Companies
3rd Signal Company
3rd Divisional Train
7th, 8th, 9th Field Ambulances

5TH DIVISION

Maj-Gen Sir C. Fergusson, Bart, CB , MVO, DSO
replaced on promotion by Maj-Gen T.L.N. Morland
18 October.

13th Infantry Brigade

Brig-Gen G.J. Cuthbert CB
2nd Bn King's Own Scottish
    Borderers
2nd Duke of Wellington's West
    Riding Regiment
1st Bn Queen's Own Royal West
    Kent Regiment
2nd Bn King's Own Yorkshire Light
    Infantry
1st Bn 9th London Regiment (TF, 27
    Nov)

15th Infantry Brigade

Brig-Gen A.E.W. Count Gleichen
    KCVO, CB, CMG, DSO
1st Bn Norfolk Regiment
1st Bn Bedfordshire Regiment
1st Bn Cheshire Regiment
1st Bn Dorsetshire Regiment

14th Infantry Brigade

Brig-Gen S.P. Rolt CB
2nd Bn Suffolk Regiment
1st Bn East Surrey Regiment
1st Bn Duke of Cornwall's Light
    Infantry
2nd Manchester Regiment

Divisional Cavalry

'A' Squadron 19th Hussars
5th Cyclist Company

Royal Engineers

Col Tulloch
17th and 59th Field Companies
5th Signal Company

5th Divisional Train
13th, 14th, 15th Field Ambulances

Royal Artillery

Brig-Gen Headlam
15th Brigade (11, 52, 80 Batteries)
27th Brigade (119, 120, 121
    Batteries)
28th Brigade (122, 123, 124
    Batteries)
8th (Howitzer) Brigade (37, 61, 65
    Batteries)
108th Heavy Battery, Royal
    Garrison Artillery

III CORPS (HQ from 29 August)

Maj-Gen W.P. Pulteney CB, DSO
Brigadier-General, General Staff: Brig-Gen J.P.
Du Cane CB

4TH DIVISION (from 25 August)

Maj-Gen T. D'O. Snow CB invalided 9 September,
replaced by Maj-Gen H.F.M. Wilson CB.

10th Infantry Brigade

Brig-Gen J.A.L. Haldane CB, DSO
    became GOC 3rd Div replaced
    by Brig-Gen Hull.
1st Bn Royal Warwickshire
    Regiment
2nd Bn Royal Warwickshire
    Regiment
2nd Bn Seaforth Highlanders
1st Royal Irish Fusiliers
2nd Bn Royal Dublin Fusiliers

11th Infantry Brigade

Brig-Gen A.G. Hunter-Weston CB,
    DSO, promoted Maj-Gen 27
    October.
1st Bn Somerset Light Infantry
1st Bn East Lancashire Regiment
1st Bn Rifle Brigade
1st Bn Hampshire Regiment
5th Bn 1st London Rifle Brigade
    (TF, 19 Nov)

12th Infantry Brigade

Brig-Gen H.F.M. Wilson CB
  became GOC 4th Div, promoted
  27 October replaced by Col F.G.
  Anley (2nd Essex).
1st Bn King's Own (Royal
  Lancaster) Regiment
2nd Bn Lancashire Fusiliers
2nd Bn Royal Inniskilling Fusiliers
2nd Bn Essex Regiment

Royal Artillery

Brig-Gen G.F. Milne
14th Brigade (39, 68, 88 Batteries)
29th Brigade (125, 126, 127
  Batteries)
32nd Brigade (27, 134, 135 Batteries)
36th Brigade (31, 35, 55 Batteries)
31st Heavy Battery, Royal Garrison
  Artillery

19th Independent Infantry Brigade (formed at Valenciennes, 22 Aug)

Maj-Gen L.G. Drummond CB,
  MVO, wounded 26 August,
  replaced by Col Ward
2nd Bn Royal Welch Fusiliers
1st Bn Scots Rifles (Cameronians)
2nd Bn Argyll and Sutherland
  Highlanders
5th Bn Cameronian Highlanders
  (TF, 19 Nov)

Divisional Cavalry

'B' Squadron 19th Hussars
4th Cyclist Company

Royal Engineers

7th and 9th Field Companies
4th Signal Company

4th Divisional Train
19th, 11th 12th Field Ambulances

6TH DIVISION (Battle of the Aisne, 16 September on)

Maj-Gen J.L. Keir CB

16th Infantry Brigade

Brig-Gen C. Ingouville-Williams CB, DSO
1st Bn East Kent Regiment (The Buffs)
1st Bn Leicestershire Regiment
1st Bn Shropshire Light Infantry
2nd Bn York and Lancaster Regiment

18th Infantry Brigade

Brig-Gen W.N. Congreve VC, CB, MVO
1st Bn West Yorkshire Regiment
1st Bn East Yorkshire Regiment
2nd Bn Durham Light Infantry
2nd Bn Notts and Derby Regiment (Sherwood Foresters)
1st Bn 16th London Regiment (TF, 11 Nov)

Royal Artillery

Brig-Gen W.L.H. Paget CB, MVO
2nd Brigade (21, 42, 53 Batteries)
24th Brigade (110, 111, 112 Batteries)
38th Brigade (24, 34, 72 Batteries)
12th (Howitzer) Brigade (43, 86, 87 Batteries)
24th Heavy Battery, Royal Garrison Artillery

17th Infantry Brigade

Brig-Gen W.R.B. Doran CB, DSO
1st Bn Royal Fusiliers
1st Bn North Staffordshire Regiment
2nd Bn Leinster Regiment
3rd Bn Rifle Brigade

Divisional Cavalry

'C' Squadron 19th Hussars
6th Cyclist Company

Royal Engineers

12th and 38th Field Companies
6th Signal Company

6th Divisional Train
16th, 17th, 18th Field Ambulances

IV CORPS (HQ 10-27 October troops originally sent to Antwerp)

Maj-Gen (Lt-Gen) Sir H.S. Rawlinson, Bart, CVO, CB
Brigadier-General, General Staff: Brig-Gen R.A.K. Montgomery CB, DSO

7TH DIVISION (landed at Ostend and Zeebrugge 6-8 October)

Maj-Gen T. Capper CB, DSO

20th Infantry Brigade

Brig-Gen H.G. Ruggles-Brise MVO, wounded 2 November, replaced by Brig-Gen F.J. Heyworth on the 14th.
1st Bn Grenadier Guards
2nd Bn Scots Guards
2nd Border Regiment
2nd Gordon Highlanders

22nd Infantry Brigade

Brig-Gen S.T.B. Lawford
2nd Bn The Queen's Royal West Surrey Regiment
2nd Bn Royal Warwickshire Regiment
1st Bn Royal Welsh Fusiliers
1st Bn South Staffordshire Regiment
8th Bn Royal Scots (TF, joined 11 Nov)

21st Infantry Brigade

Brig-Gen H.E. Watts CB
2nd Bn Bedfordshire Regiment
2nd Bn Yorkshire Regiment
2nd Bn Wiltshire Regiment
2nd Bn Royal Scots Fusiliers

Divisional Cavalry

Northumberland Yeomanry
7th Cyclist Company

Royal Engineers

54th and 55th Field Companies
7th Signal Company

7th Divisional Train
21st, 22nd, 23rd Field Ambulances

Royal Artillery

'F' and 'T' RHA Batteries (14th
   Brigade)
22nd Brigade (104, 105, 106
   Batteries)
25th Brigade (12, 35, 58 Batteries)
3rd Brigade, 111th, 112th Heavy
   Batteries (4.7in) RGA

3RD CAVALRY DIVISION (reached Ypres 14 October)

Maj-Gen Hon J.H.G. Byng CB, MVO

6th Cavalry Brigade

Brig-Gen E. Makins DSO
1st Dragoons (Royals)
10th Hussars
3rd Dragoon Guards (joined 4 Nov)
North Somerset Yeomanry
   (attached 13 Nov)

Royal Horse Artillery

'C' and 'K' Batteries (15th Brigade)
   plus 'G' Battery (25 Nov)

7th Cavalry Brigade

Brig-Gen C.T. McM Kavanagh
   CVO, CB, DSO
1st Life Guards
2nd Life Guards
Royal Horse Guards (Blues)
Leicestershire Yeomanry (joined 12
   Nov)

Royal Engineers

3rd Field Squadron
3rd Signal Squadron

6th, 7th, 8th Cavalry Field
   Ambulances

INDIAN CORPS (began relieving II Corps 23 October)

Lt-Gen Sir James Willcocks GCMG, KCB, KCSI, DSO
Brigadier-General, General Staff: Brig-Gen H. Hudson CB

LAHORE DIVISION (began landing at Marseilles 26 Sept)

Lt-Gen H.B.B. Watkis CB

Ferozepore Brigade

Brig-Gen R.M. Egerton CB
1st Bn Connaught Rangers
57th Indian (Wilde's) Rifles
9th Bhopal Infantry
129th Baluchi Regiment

Sirhind Brigade

1st Bn Highland Light Infantry
1st Bn 1st King George's Own
   Gurkha Rifles
1st Bn 4th Gurkha Rifles
125th Napier's Rifles

Royal Artillery

Brig-Gen H.F. Mercer CB, ADC
5th Brigade (64, 73, 81 Batteries)
11th Brigade (83, 84, 85 Batteries)
18th Brigade (59, 93, 94 Batteries)
109th Heavy Battery (4.7in) RGA

Jullundur Brigade

Maj-Gen P.M. Carnegy CB
1st Bn Manchester Regiment
15th Ludhiana Sikh Regiment
47th Sikh Regiment
59th Scinde Rifles (Frontier Force)

Divisional Cavalry

15th Lancers (Cureton's Multanis)

Engineers

20th and 21st Companies, 3rd
   Sappers and Miners
Lahore Signal Company
34th Sikh Pioneers

Lahore Divisional Train
7th and 8th British, 111th, 112th, and
   113th Indian Field Ambulances

MEERUT DIVISION

Lt-Gen C.A. Anderson CB

Dehra Dun Brigade

Brig-Gen C.E. Johnson
1st Bn Seaforth Highlanders
1st Bn 9th Gurkha Rifles
2nd Bn 2nd King Edward's Own
    Gurkha Rifles (Sirmoor Rifles)
6th Jat Light Infantry

Bareilly Brigade

Maj-Gen F. Macbean CVO, CB
2nd Bn Black Watch
41st Dogra Regiment
58th Rifles (Frontier Force)
2nd Bn 8th Gurkha Rifles

Royal Artillery

Brig-Gen A.B. Scott CB, DSO
4th Brigade (7, 14, 66 Batteries)
9th Brigade (19, 20, 28 Batteries)
13th Brigade (2, 8, 44 Batteries)
110th Heavy Battery, RGA

Garhwal Brigade

Maj-Gen H. D'U. Keary CB, DSO
2nd Bn Leicester Regiment
2nd Bn 3rd Queen Alexandra's Own
    Gurkha Rifles
1st and 2nd Bns Garhwal Rifles

Engineers

3rd and 4th Companies, 1st King
    George's Own Sappers and
    Miners
Meerut Signal Company

Divisional Cavalry

4th Cavalry Regiment

Meerut Divisional Train
19th and 20th British, 128th
129th and 130th Indian Field
Ambulances

Secunderabad Cavalry Brigade (arrived in France 12 October)

Brig-Gen F.W.G. Wadeson
7th Dragoon Guards
34th Poona Horse
20th Deccan Horse
'N' Battery RHA
1st Indian Field Troop
Jodhpore Imperial Service Lancers (attached)

By 30 November Indian Corps losses totalled 292 British and Indian officers
    killed, wounded or missing and 5659 other ranks out of a fighting strength
    of about 30,000 men.

ROYAL FLYING CORPS

Brig-Gen Sir D. Henderson KCB, DSO (promoted
Maj-Gen 27 Oct)

2nd, 3rd, 4th and 5th Aeroplane Squadrons (plus 6th
in action by 16 Oct)
1st Aircraft Park

Note: This order of battle lists formations heavily engaged up to the
end of November. The 8th (Regular) Division arrived in France on 6
November but only its leading brigade (the 23rd) saw much action
(with the Cavalry Corps) from 11 November, suffering 541 casualties.
Army and Line of Communication units are not included.

Appendix C

FRENCH AND GERMAN ARMIES
August – November 1914

FRENCH ARMY after mobilisation

Joffre

FIRST ARMY
Dubail
280,000 men (16 divs)
VII, VIII, XIII, XIV, XXI Corps
44th Inf Div
3 res divs
Alpine Gp
2 cav divs

minus VII and XXI Corps

minus IX and XV Corps
minus 1 cav div
plus 1 res div

SECOND ARMY
De Castelnau
180,000 men (14½ divs)
IX, XV, XVI, XX Corps
mixed colonial bde
3 res divs
2 cav divs

During Battle of the Marne

Sarrail
minus IV Corps and 42nd Div (VI Corps)
plus XV Corps
plus 1 res div

THIRD ARMY
Ruffey
200,000 men (11 divs)
IV, V, VI Corps
3 res divs
1 cav div

FOURTH ARMY
Langle de Cary
160,000 men (14 divs)
II, XI, XII, XVII, Colonial Corps
2 res divs
1 cav div

minus XI Corps
plus XXI corps
minus 2 res divs
minus 1 cav dir

FIFTH ARMY
Lanrezac
240,000 men (17 divs)
I, III, X, XVIII Corps
37th and 38th Inf Divs
2 res divs
4 cav divs

Franchet d'Esperey
unchanged

SIXTH ARMY
Maunoury
150,000 men (9 divs)
IV and VII Corps
45th Inf Div
4 res divs

NINTH ARMY (9 divs)
Foch
IX and XI Corps
42nd Inf Div
2 res divs
1 cav div

TENTH ARMY formed north of Arras early October
de Maud'huy

EIGHTH ARMY formed for Ypres sector
d'Urbal
By 11 Nov IX, XVI, XX, XXI, 8 cav divs, 1 marine bde

Note: Corps comprised 2 divs except VI and the Colonial Corps which had 3 divs.

GERMAN ARMY

von Moltke

FIRST ARMY
von Kluck
260,000 men (18½ divs)
II, III, IV, IX Corps
III, IV, IX Res Corps
3 *Landwehr* bdes
3 cav divs

minus III and IX Res Corps to besiege Antwerp.

SECOND ARMY
von Bülow
260,000 men (15 divs)
Guard, VII, X Corps
Guard, VII, X Res Corps
2 *Landwehr* bdes
2 cav divs

minus Gd Res Corps to E Front from 26 Aug, and VII Res Corps to besiege Maubeuge till 8 Sept.

THIRD ARMY
von Hausen
120,000 men (8½ divs)
XI, XII and XIX Saxon Corps
XII Saxon Res Corps
1 *Landwehr* bde

minus XI Corps to E Front from 26 Aug.

FOURTH ARMY
Albrecht of Würtemberg
200,000 men (10½ divs)
VIII and XVIII Corps
VIII and XVIII Res corps
1 *Landwehr* bde

FIFTH ARMY
Crown Prince
200,000 men (17¾ divs)
V, VI, XIII, XXI Corps
V and VI Res Corps
33rd Res Div
5 *Landwehr* bdes
2 cav divs

SIXTH ARMY
Rupert of Bavaria
200,000 men (17½ divs)
I, II, III Bav, XXI Corps
I Bav Res Corps
4 *Ersatz* divs
1 *Landwehr* bde
3 cav divs

SEVENTH ARMY
von Heeringen
120,000 men (9½ divs)
XIV and XV Corps
XIV Res Corps
Strassburg Res Div
2 *Ersatz* divs
1 *Landwehr* bde

XXII, XXIII, XXVI, XXVII Res Corps were at the front by October for the Flanders offensive forming a reconstituted FOURTH ARMY with III Reserve Corps, 2 reserve divisions and a German Navy Marine Division. SIXTH ARMY HQ by 20 October controlled its original cavalry among 8 divisions reorganised in 4 corps, II, II Bavarian, VII, XIII, XV, XIX Saxon Corps with XIV Reserve Corps and 11th *Landwehr* Brigade. Four Guards regiments formed Winckler's Composite Division for the 11 November attack.

Appendix D

A NOTE ON CASUALTIES

Only the BEF casualties in 1914 can be determined with any exactitude.
Mons (23-24 August) 4352 killed, wounded and missing, 2 guns.
Le Cateau (26 August) 7812 killed wounded and missing (2600 prisoners) and 36 guns.
Total for the retreat 15,000 and 42 guns.
Battle of the Marne 1700.
Battle of the Aisne 561 officers and 12,980 men.
First Battle of Ypres (14 October–30 November) 2368 officers and 55,787 men.

This total of just under 90,000 was equivalent to the entire original BEF. Only an average of 1 officer and 30 men remained of each of the original 64 thousand-strong battalions landed in France during August.

French Army casualties for August alone (only 12 days of major fighting) totalled 4478 officers and 206,515 other ranks of which more than two thirds were sustained in the *five* days of the Battle of the Frontiers (20-24 August). These precise figures exclude Territorial and garrison units. No separate figures exist for the Battle of the Marne but a grand total of 300,000 is generally accepted for the first two months of the war, together with another 50,000 during First Ypres.

Belgian Army losses for the first four months of the war are hard to isolate but a figure of 50,000 of which at least a quarter were prisoners from Liège, Namur and Antwerp seems a reasonable guesstimate.

German losses are even harder to pin down and have never been officially compiled in full. Two set of *Reichsarchiv* figures for Flanders alone (13/15 October – 24 November) come to totals of 123,910 and 134,315. Perhaps 400,000 Germans fell on the Western Front in the first four months.

BIBLIOGRAPHY

Arthur, Sir George, *Kitchener,* Volume III (Macmillan, 1920)

Baker-Carr, C.D., *From Chauffeur to Brigadier-General* (Ernest Benn, 1930)

Bishop, Christopher and Ellis, John, *Vehicles at War* (Allen & Unwin, 1979)

Buchan, John, *A History of the Great War* (Nelson, 1921-22)

Burrows, John W., *History of the Essex Regiment* (John H. Burrows & Sons Ltd., Basildon, 1927)

Childers, Spencer, *Hugh Childers* (John Murray, 1901)

Creasy, Sir Edward, *The Fifteen Decisive Battles of the World* (London, 1851)

Edmonds, Brigadier-General Sir James, *History of the Great War, based on Official Documents, Military Operations France and Belgium 1914* (London, 1922)

Farwell, Byron, *Queen Victoria's Little Wars* (Allen Lane, 1973)

French, Field-Marshal Viscount, *1914* (Constable, 1919) *The Despatches of Lord French* (London, 1917)

Fuller, Major-General J.F.C., *The Conduct of War 1789-1961* (Eyre & Spottiswoode, 1961)

Fussell, Paul, *The Great War and Modern Memory* (OUP, 1975)

Glubb, Sir John, *Into Battle: A Soldier's Diary of the Great War* (Cassell, 1977)

Hanotaux, Gabriel, *Histoire illustrée de la guerre de 1914. L'Enigme de Charleroi* (Paris, 1916)

Holmes, Richard, *The Little Field-Marshal – Sir John French* (Jonathan Cape, 1981)

Keegan, John and Wheatcroft, Andrew, *Who's Who in Military History* (Weidenfeld & Nicholson, 1976)

Kluck, Colonel-General Alexander von, *The March on Paris 1914* (Edward Arnold, 1920)

Liddell Hart, Captain Basil H., *The Real War* (Cassell, 1930)

Ludendorff, General Erich, *My War Memories* Volume I (Hutchinson, 1921)

Magnus, Philip, *Kitchener: Portrait of an Imperialist* (London, 1961)

Marshall-Cornwall, General Sir James, *Foch as Military Commander* (Batsford, 1972)

Mason, Philip, *A Matter of Honour* (Jonathan Cape, 1974)

Maurice, Major-General Sir Frederick, *Forty Days in 1914* (2nd edition, Constable, 1920)

Palmer, Alan, *The Kaiser: Warlord of the Second Reich* (Weidenfeld & Nicolson, 1977)

Raleigh, Sir Walter, *Official History of the War in the Air*, Volume I (Oxford Clarendon Press, 1922)

Robertson, Field-Marshal Sir William, *From Private to Field-Marshal* (London, 1921)

Smithers, A.J., *The Man Who Disobeyed, Sir Horace Smith-Dorrien and His Enemies* (Leo Cooper, 1970) *'Toby', A Real Life Ripping Yarn* (Gordon & Cremonesi, 1978)

Spears, Brigadier-General Edward L., *Liaison 1914* (Eyre & Spottiswoode, 1930)

Terraine, John, *Mons – Retreat to Victory* (Batsford, 1960) *Douglas Haig, The Educated Soldier* (London, 1963) *The Smoke and The Fire: Myths and Anti-Myths of War* (Sidgwick & Jackson, 1980) *White Heat: The New Warfare 1914-18* (Sidgwick & Jackson, 1982)

Willcocks Sir James, *With the Indians in France* (Constable & Co, 1925)

Whitton, F.E. *The Marne Campaign* (Constable & Co, 1925)

Windrow, Martin and Mason, David, *A Concise Dictionary of Military Biography* (Osprey, 1975)

INDEX

185

188